Voice from the Desert

VOICE
FROM
~THE~
DESERT

A BISHOP'S CRY FOR A NEW CHURCH

Bishop Jacques Gaillot

Translated by Joseph Cunneen & Léon King

A Crossroad Book
The Crossroad Publishing Company
New York

1996
The Crossroad Publishing Company
370 Lexington Avenue, New York, NY 10017

Copyright © 1995 by Éditions Albin Michel S.A.—Paris
English translation copyright © 1996 by
The Crossroad Publishing Company

Printed in the United States of America

Library of Congress Cataloging-in-Publication Data

Gaillot, Jacques, 1935–
  [Chers amis de Partenia— . English]
  Voice from the desert : a bishop's cry for a new church / Jacques
Gaillot : translated by Joseph Cunneen and Léon King.
     p. cm.
  ISBN 0-8245-1584-6
  1. Catholic Church—Controversial literature. 2. Imaginary
letters. 3. Gaillot, Jacques, 1935–   . 4. Catholic Church—
Pastoral letters and charges. 5. Catholic Church—France—
History—20th century. 6. France—Moral conditions. 7. France—
Social conditions—1945– 8. France—church history—1945–
I. Title.
BX1779.5.G3513   1996
282'.09'049–dc20   96-23244
                                                        CIP

"Some day, when you finally
can't put up with any more,
you will resign. And you will go
to wash the feet of the poor,
embrace the lepers, and
visit the prisoners.
It is they who are
Jesus Christ."
— *Letter from a priest*

Contents

FOREWORD

Thomas C. Fox

FRENCH BISHOP JACQUES GAILLOT had no idea, when called to appear before Cardinal Bernardin Gantin of the Congregation of Bishops at the Vatican, on January 12, 1995, how much was at stake. No bishop in modern history had been summarily dismissed from his see.

The then 59-year-old Gaillot recalls that his first shock, on arriving at Gantin's office, was to find himself flanked by two other prelates, an Argentinean archbishop and Msgr. Jean-Louis Tauran, a Frenchman. Some months earlier a bishop had warned Gaillot to "beware of Tauran." But it was now too late.

"We need to have a serious talk," Gantin led off. The hard-line Vatican conservative then began recounting a history he had compiled of what he called Gaillot's "case." It included a list of references to earlier warnings and subsequent "inappropriate" behavior, at least from Rome's vantage, on the part of the bishop from Évreux.

One exchange: "You declared that the word of God is a word like any other," Gantin charged.

"What I meant was that in today's culture the word of God often means no more than any other," Gaillot responded.

What followed then was a litany of other Vatican complaints, including matters such as failing to notify other bishops when visiting their dioceses, not adequately depicting official Catholic teachings while appearing on French television, and advocating the use of condoms to prevent the spreading of the HIV virus. In each instance there was not much to discuss. Gaillot was not given time for explanation. The script for the meeting, it appeared in retrospect, had long been written, judgments had been made, and a verdict, signed by the pope, then traveling in the Philippines, was already in hand.

Gantin ended the session abruptly with a stark demand. He wanted Gaillot's immediate resignation. When the bishop refused, Gantin announced bluntly: "It has been decided that tomorrow you should retire as bishop of Évreux. At noon. And the Diocese of Évreux will be declared vacant."

Gaillot was stunned. Never, as he traveled to Rome for what he thought would be an uncomfortable meeting with Gantin, had he remotely expected such an ultimatum. When Gaillot again balked, the Vatican prelate simply handed him a note signed by the Supreme Pontiff only days before, confirming the deed. There had been no official judicial hearing, no process, no consultation with the French episcopal conference. If any French prelates knew in advance what was to occur they never shared the knowledge. The reason Gantin gave for the action was that Gaillot had ceased being "in communion with the church." The next day, the Vatican issued a statement announcing Gaillot's ouster. It said in part that "he failed to exercise his episcopal ministry in doctrinal and pastoral union with the church."

Word reached the *National Catholic Reporter* newsroom in Kansas City, Missouri, within hours. Calls from France. Several wire services. The editors were also stunned. During the hard-line pontificate of Pope John Paul II, a reaction to the renewal-minded pontificates of Pope John XXIII and Pope Paul VI, Vatican moves against allegedly wayward Catholics had been commonplace. Some of the church's most creative thinkers, including its best pastors and most noted theologians, had been treated poorly by zealous Roman prelates who, in the name of a self-proclaimed orthodoxy, had humiliated and marginalized Catholics, many who had given their entire lives to the church. The Vatican during John Paul II's pontificate had moved against Catholics such as Hans Küng, Leonardo Boff, Raymond Hunthausen, Bill Callahan, Matthew Fox, Edwina Gately, Robert Nugent,

Jeannine Grammick, Richard McBrien, Charles Curran, and Ivone Gebara—but never with the speed or severity it moved against Bishop Jacques Gaillot.

The reaction to the Vatican action was equally swift— and widespread. Catholics both in France and throughout much of Europe and North America protested loudly.

"I regret this decision," said the French archbishop of Cambrai, Jacques Delaporte. "For our church, it is a wound. For dialogue, it is a failure. For the poor and those seeking a direction who put their confidence in him [Gaillot], it is a source of incomprehension. . . . If mission and communion do not go together, we are moving sooner or later toward a clash," he said.

Bishop Jean Vilnet of Lille called the Vatican's decision "extremely grave." It is thanks to Gaillot that "the poor, the marginal, the excluded, those seeking hope, felt understood, supported, recognized," he said.

President of the French bishops' conference, Archbishop Joseph Duval of Rouen, said: "I am sad. I never ceased to hope that we would not be faced with such a situation. I am sad for Bishop Gaillot, for the Diocese of Évreux. I am sad for the church." Several French bishops publicly asked for a gathering of the entire episcopal conference.

Clearly Gaillot had his detractors among the French bishops, but the sacking was widely viewed as excessive. Only Cardinal Jean-Marie Lustiger of Paris was initially known to actively support the move.

Le Monde, the prestigious French daily, several days after the sacking carried six articles about Gaillot. In one front-page article, the paper said the church was "distancing itself from society." Other French papers played up the story as well. A French bishop told *NCR* the effect of the move would be precisely opposite to what Rome had wanted, drawing more attention to Gaillot's thinking, while giving the bishop new celebrity status. It would even free him from his immediate ecclesial responsibilities and allow his voice to be heard even more widely. From the vast outpouring of commentary in the French media, one serious and unsettling theme emerged—a gap was growing between the Vatican and many French Catholics.

That week I wrote an editorial that began: "The Vatican significantly raised the stakes last week in the ecclesial debate on the use—and abuse—of authority. . . . The reason Gantin gave for the action was that Gaillot was not in communion with the church. French Catholics and others were asking: Who was not in communion with the church?"

As news of action spread, rallies and protests erupted throughout France. Within two days, Gaillot had received more than 1,000 telegrams and faxes expressing support. In the French city of Metz, parish priests refused to preach at Sunday Mass the following week. Within hours, Gaillot's removal was taking its toll on the French church. He had been a popular and articulate figure, a cleric. He had spoken out on behalf of the poor and the marginalized. He knew the media. He used it well. His message was always one of understanding and compassion. Later Gaillot noted, "They can't muzzle someone. . . . Now that I have become an outsider of sorts, perhaps my determination will be even more vigorous than before. . . . I will not keep silent."

Within days of the removal, nine German theologians, including Hans Küng, released a "telegram of solidarity." "We protest resolutely against this arbitrary action by the papacy. It involves a bishop who, following Jesus in discipleship and motivated by pastoral responsibility, exercised his office as the gospel demands with extraordinary openness and readiness to enter into dialogue."

Between 15,000 and 20,000 attended Gaillot's farewell Mass in Évreux, about 55 miles from Paris. Many huddled outside the Cathedral of Notre Dame in the pouring rain. The Mass was concelebrated by many priests and four other French bishops; among those attending were Catholic delegations from Germany, Switzerland, and Belgium.

"You have given me so much happiness," began Gaillot's message, read that day in all churches of the diocese. "I ask forgiveness of those to whom I caused suffering. . . . The moment has come to leave you. Some will be sorry. Others will rejoice. The important thing is to follow Christ. . . . Welcome whoever is sent as pastor of the Church of Évreux."

Gaillot had long shown an independent streak, defending homosexuals, urging a married priesthood, speaking up loudly for the unemployed and homeless of France. In 1993, he had come out in support of a proposed French law to recognize same-sex unions. He reportedly once recited a prayer of "welcome" for a gay couple. In an October 1992 edition of *Gai Pied*, a now-defunct French publication dealing with homosexual concerns, he explained that he had received a request from a gay couple to bless their marriage. "Please receive us, although we are pariahs of the church," he said the couple had asked him. "I've got AIDS. My life will soon come to an end. Therefore, we would very much like you to bless our union. It would be such a comfort." Gaillot said he agreed to meet the couple and "to say a prayer, a sign of welcome and understanding."

Not long after the Vatican action against Gaillot, it began to become clear to many church observers Rome had miscalculated the effect of the firing. First, there were the thousands who showed up for his farewell Mass. Then there was the continuing coverage by the French press, including that of one Rome correspondent for the Catholic *La Croix*, who reported that the Vatican was being deluged with mail addressed to Pope John Paul II and Gantin— protesting the treatment of Gaillot. Finally there was the French bishops' conference itself. Citing Gaillot's dedication to Christ, the conference announced it would continue his salary and benefits, even while supporting the Vatican's decision. Months later, Cardinal Lustiger of Paris acknowledged the Gaillot controversy had revealed serious internal divisions in French Catholicism and "a split between generations."

In late 1995, almost one year after the Vatican move, Pope John Paul II and Gaillot met at the Vatican for the first time face to face. Following a thirty-minute encounter, Gaillot, who had been living in a community of the homeless in central Paris, said he was convinced that the pope wanted to "turn the page" and clarify his standing in the church. "I hope to continue to express and witness to the Gospel's liberating message, while remaining in communion with the church," Gaillot said.

The following month, Gaillot marked the first anniversary of his ouster by turning his newly assigned but non-existing titular see of Partenia, a long defunct see in the middle of the Sahara Desert, into the world's first cyber-diocese by putting it on the World Wide Web. He said it would be a "place of liberty" open to all. Gaillot's site (www.partenia.fr) is modest in comparison with the Vatican's own web page, which started one month earlier, but in going onto the global electronic web, Gaillot let it be known he wanted to reach out to all Catholics who, like himself, had become "homeless" in the church. In the wake of the Gaillot matter, that number was rising.

Thomas C. Fox is editor and associate publisher of the National Catholic Reporter.

1 ～

I come to you today...

Dear friends in Partenia,

I don't know whether you will be offended when I say this, but at first many people didn't take your existence seriously. It's not anyone's fault. Your name sounds like an ancient costume, a reminder of the Roman conquest, and there aren't many centurions around these days. All the same, and in spite of my reputed sense of humor, I wasn't thinking about a joke. Not this time.

Twelve years ago, I didn't believe it at first when I heard that I had been appointed bishop of Évreux, a small town fifty-five miles northwest of Paris. I was younger then, with less of a weight on my shoulders, and I was only convinced after carefully reading the letter on my desk, a communication that bore the seal of the nunciature. This time, however, even without the letter, it never occurred to me to doubt for an instant. This certitude proceeded from Rome, from where I had returned, and from three prelate-judges who, the night before, had not even for a moment appeared to be people who loved a hoax.[1]

The geographical conclusion to the affair was slightly more uncanny. Although even before all this happened . . .

Don't take further offense, dear friends, but it has been centuries since Partenia appeared on the surface of the globe; in the modern world, I am told, it isn't even mentioned on quiz shows. However, ignorance doesn't rule out impatience. For days, in public and in the press, people groped with maps and globes, ready to put their finger on the modest spot. I wasn't the only one to flounder; the Larousse dictionary had informed me about Évreux, but in this instance I was on my own . . .

It was first thought I had been "transferred" to Parthenay, in the Deux-Sèvres, to the great joy of a nephew whose neighbor

---

1. They were Cardinal Bernardin Gantin, prefect of the Congregation of Bishops; Cardinal Jean-Louis Tauran, secretary of the Congregation; and the Argentine Archbishop Jorge Mejía, Vatican secretary for foreign relations.

I would have become. Then Partenia appeared to be exiled in Mauritania in present-day west Africa, buried in the sands of the desert. It was finally located on a map dating from the fifth century, that a few scholars in geography had dusted off, of Christian North Africa, an area then called Mauretania (with an *e*, unlike the later Mauritania, with an *i*).

It is understandable, therefore, that we've had some difficulty in getting together again. Time's forgetfulness has made you a vanished, invisible people, a mythical island that sank into the sea, a sort of Atlantis of the faith. Your name, today bracketed with mine, reappears out of the depths of history like a disastrous mirage, a sombre chimera that has emerged from a bogey-man's basket. But it so happens that for me you really exist. For me, it's not a question of place or dimension or history. You are neither a phantom nor a lost diocese, still less a diocese to be reestablished. Indeed, you're not really a diocese at all. For me, friends of Partenia, you are the world. Wherever you are, whether in a Moslem land or elsewhere, in prisons or living rooms, at my door or thousands of miles away. The kind of world I love, with a vast horizon, without shackles or barriers. A world for men and women, a world for the Gospel. That's the way I see it. A spot that's everywhere and nowhere. And this is how I see you as I come to you today.

People will tell you that I am taking this trip under duress. It's true. Frankly, I would not have thought of Partenia all by myself. But I can also claim to have had a choice in the matter. Under the cover of a voluntary resignation, they proposed that I remain at Évreux with the title of bishop emeritus—in other words, as honorary bishop, detached from the structure. To tell the truth, I don't deserve any credit for refusing. I like the rose bushes in the bishop's garden, but not to the point of wanting to prune them all day. I therefore chose to be a "transferred" bishop. It is, undoubtedly, an ugly title, with an authoritarian resonance, but at least it has the charm of the unknown. I didn't really know what it meant, what it had to do with being a bishop . . .

It is only fair to make it clear that, in the eyes of Vatican archaeologists, you are neither a distinction nor a prize. And certainly not a promotion. They dipped into their reserves, and found there a bad mark to accompany the punishment I received from the Roman prelates. Let's admit it right away: I am the object of a "fraternal correction." A bishop that has been punished, a rare product . . . in addition to being, according to the official communiqué, an incompetent bishop.

There was not the smallest trace of a blue sky in the cold, tense atmosphere in which my judges performed their task. One can have individual conscience and a faith pegged to the body, but to learn in less than half an hour that after twelve years of pastoral responsibilities you have not shown yourself qualified to "exercise the ministry of unity which is a bishop's first duty," and that, "in consideration of this, we have decided that tomorrow, beginning at noon, you will be relieved of your responsibilities at Évreux," can be a sharp blow to one's confidence. I confess without shame that in the hours that followed, the name Partenia appeared to me to be an extra blow, a faraway land lost in the mists of oblivion, a place of exile marked with the seal of infamy.

Will you forgive me, dear friends of Partenia, for this temporary emotional and disillusioned reaction? I no longer feel that way.

I no longer feel that way because, as Martin Luther King said, "I have a dream"—that I will be able to bring the word of the Gospel to everyone everywhere. My dream is to be able to get right into the middle of things, to go out on the street, to play a role in the media and other places that may have been corrupted, without any fear of being charged with keeping bad company. To be able to go out without worrying about whether I'm in my own back yard or am infringing on the territory of one of my colleagues. To no longer have to fear the ire of the Holy See because—and I quote—"of my frequent trips outside my diocese." My diocese? Partenia has no boundaries . . .

"No constraint in religion"

I HAD A DREAM: to be able to accompany the poor, the excluded, the ignored, without having to explain myself or justify myself to the rich, the secure, or the comfortable. To be able to go where distress calls me without having to give advance notice. To be able to show my indignation at destitution, injustice, violence, the sale of weapons, and managed famines without being considered a meddler in politics.

I dreamed of being able to live my faith within the church, but also in society, in my time and with my times. I dreamed of the freedom to think and express myself, to debate and criticize, without fear of the guillotine. I dreamed of being different within the unity of faith, and remaining myself, alone and yet in solidarity with others. Ultimately, I hoped to be able to proclaim a Gospel of freedom without being marginalized. . .

I had a dream, and that dream became reality. "The pope has done you a great service," someone wrote me. "You are going to be able to leave your palace, and live off Christ, living with him, where he is . . . " Apart from the fact that my episcopal residence at Évreux was not a palace, my correspondent is correct: By liberating me against my wishes, Rome offers me more than I dared to hope for, much more than a diocese, much more than a bishopric. It offers me Partenia—to me, who previously had been asked to jog only between the rue Saint-Louis and the cathedral, who was accused of seeing, listening, and speaking far beyond my authorized limits, who was reproached for acting as a lone ranger on unknown shores that were considered contagious, Rome now offers me a hundred, a thousand times more. It gives me blanket permission, it allows me to breathe, it offers me liberation. Questions like where is Partenia, what is it, when did it exist, are pointless. Partenia is a phantom that goes through walls, passes over many lands, and crosses oceans. It cuts through protocol, intolerance, and prejudices. As vast as the world, Partenia does not begin or end anywhere. Even though I didn't look for it, the destination suits me, and that's where I'm going.

You will undoubtedly be surprised to learn that you were part of my plans long ago. As a young seminarian, I was hoping to serve in a foreign mission, somewhere in the Middle East. At the age of twenty-six, after becoming a priest, this was still my intention, but the bishop of Langres decided he needed me in his diocese. He kept me in France.

Meanwhile, my youthful existence was drastically changed by an experience that has greatly influenced what I have become—and will influence me for the rest of my life. It was a brutal shock in which, quite involuntarily, you played an important part . . .

For, you see, this is not my first "transfer" to what was once known as the ancient kingdom of Mauretania Sitifenis, which we locate today in a deserted area of Algeria. Almost forty years ago now, I was ordered to go there, in the same authoritarian way. The uniform was not the same, and the mission was far more dismal, with no connection to evangelism. It was in 1957, I was not yet twenty-two years old, and they ordered me to take up arms—which, needless to say, seemed to me incompatible with my religious vocation—in order to defend the French presence in Algeria. I had to pass back and forth many times over the land of Partenia. I didn't just pass by there; I stayed twenty-four months. Far from the family nest and the protective institutions of the church. "In the middle of a hurricane," as I often told myself, "and completely on my own."

But unarmed: Named an officer in the specialized administrative section, assigned to the prefect of Sétif, given the job of pacification in a zone that covered fifty square miles, I served the local population, looking after passes and schools, the sick, prisoners, and the missing. By making myself useful in this way, I resolved my personal problem, but if I was not exactly in the front row, I had a fine seat in a side box for judging the frightful destruction that accompanies a war. I observed the panic of a population that was used as a hostage by both camps; the metamorphosis of ordinary young people who, under the pressure of events, became degraded and transformed into wild beasts; an atmosphere of fear, hatred, and violence; constantly open wounds in flesh and spirit; torture and repression.

I realize today that it was there, in the vicinity of Partenia, that something was triggered in me: my complete rejection of all recourse to violence, my support for and commitment to every type of peaceful struggle. The corollary to this was my profound conviction, which has constantly grown deeper within me ever since, that nonviolence is the only force, the only genuine defense of the poor.

I also know that it was there, around Partenia, that I experienced the shift from a received faith to an interiorized faith.

I have kept many strong memories of that period. And also some concrete ties. I have not lost touch with some friends, with whom I correspond regularly, even today . . . And now, more than thirty-five years later, life sends me back to them as a new bishop in Algeria.

Moslem brothers, it is a Christian who approaches you. I come with sentiments of peace. I know that the veil of blood that descends on you today is not that of true Islamic faith, which orders neither crime nor intolerance. I also know that you, inhabitants of Kabylia, are people who reject that criminal direction. I always tell Christians not to be afraid of other religions, not to be afraid of differences. To you, brother Moslems, I offer a symbolic word taken from the Qur'an. Tradition has it that a bishop chooses a coat of arms and a motto for his new diocese. Since I was not drawn to aristocratic imagery, I didn't follow that practice at Évreux.

Even today I scarcely feel the need of boosting my rank or of taking up arms, even decorative ones. But I'd like these words from the Qur'an (Sura 2, verse 256) to be my motto, and to become a fraternal link between us:

"No coercion in matters of religion"

I am the stranger asking for your hospitality. I know that we are different, and people say that our faith separates us from each other. But couldn't it, on the contrary, bring us closer together because of the love that it embodies? It is true, nevertheless, that I have been sent to you like someone with the plague—who must be banished at all costs. Are you willing to welcome me? Will you accept a bishop who has been reprimanded, "transferred," demoted? A homeless bishop, one who has no permanent diocese? I come empty-handed, without ornaments. I left my staff and miter in the Évreux cathedral, and I don't miss them. My friends have always made fun of me for traveling with very little baggage, whatever the symbols.

You don't know anything about me; I'm asking for your trust and your confidence. You don't know anything, that is, unless news or rumors about your bishop have reached you, accusing him of being a source of shame and scandal, a rebel and a troublemaker. Or perhaps you have heard pleas on behalf of a stubborn mule of the Gospel who, like so many others, suffers when he sees the church adopting "ready-made" thinking and growing hardened in its principles and morality?

Dear friends in Partenia, Christians and Moslems, Jews and nonbelievers, I come in an effort to live in brotherhood. Toward you and with you, I will be simply "Jacques"; I don't want my office to be a hindrance to dialogue. I will try to conduct myself among you without hidden motives, without placing the mask of the prelate between us, which would allow me to hide at will behind the official language of the institution.

That said, if some of you insist on calling me "Father," you should do so, though Jesus warns us against the name and rejects it even for himself. But whether you address me as father, or most reverend—the way bishops have been addressed down through the centuries—or Jacques, the important thing is for you to speak to me and not to the institutional authority that I am supposed to represent.

THE YEARS I SPENT at Évreux were important and beautiful years of ministry. It was a rich adventure with the Gospel, filled with wonderful times and severe trials. I retain a happy memory of the one and no bitterness about the other. I wanted to remain myself, to be an activist in a church which would be open to the future, and which would not succumb to the temptation to withdraw into its shell. A church with a human face, a more tolerant and less cold church, without taboos and prohibitions.

I have been brought down. But because of my fall, thousands of other Christians, who for far too long had lost hope, are picking themselves up. Thanks to them, nothing is over yet. The road is not closed. Someone told me one day, "Take risks, endure blows, but don't be silent." I will not be silent. There will be neither rupture nor abdication. You are going to hear from me, friends in Partenia. It's all going to continue. With you. Wherever you are.

2 ᶜ᷎

If Partenia's story were told . . .

THE STORY CAN, if you like, be told as a tale. Once upon a time, in the age of triumphal Christendom on African soil, there was Partenia. A cross planted in "Sitifian Mauretania," on the mountains of Kabylia, some 150 miles east of present-day Algiers. A modest cross, lost in the dust of bishoprics hardly larger than the parishes which covered North Africa at that time. Practically nothing is known of the diocese—neither the date of its foundation nor its exact location—which is hardly important for someone who doesn't care very much about boundaries. According to specialists, Partenia is cited only once in ancient history, in the year 484, when Huneric, king of the Vandals and invader of this part of Africa, summoned the bishops to his palace in Carthage. Under the pretext of ironing out the problems between the local church and the clergy that he brought along with him as part of his baggage, Huneric persecuted and scattered the local prelates. Among the exiled was Rogatus of Partenia.

It is a dark tale. In fact, it took place at the end of a bitter conflict that inflamed the church and that whole part of North Africa during the fourth century. That was a long time ago, you will say. But, unfortunately, it is a great deal less buried in the catacombs of history than it appears. For this "affair" already brought into play two fundamental questions: tolerance and secularism. This makes it worth the trouble to take a trip on a time machine. What was it all about? Installed in his African fiefdom, Bishop Donatus, and along with him those who supported the Donatist heresy, rejected the authority of the bishops who, at the time of the persecutions of Diocletian, had agreed to give the holy scriptures to the Romans who occupied the area. Over time, the conflict between the "pure and harsh" Donatists and the Catholic Church, which had pardoned former "traitors," became more and more bitter, giving rise to memorable theological struggles in which each party appealed to God and the authentic tradition of the church. A climate of hatred and resentment followed, leading finally to civil war. When Saint Augustine became bishop of Hippo, the violence was at its height, and the Donatists, invoking the tradition of the martyrs, exalted the spirit of sacrifice, and increased the number of their murders and ritual suicides. Obsessed by what they considered to be purity, these narrow-minded extremists refused to obey the descendants of those who had soiled their hands by compromising with pagans. They tried desperately to build, even at the price of bloodshed, a church of "saints." Does that remind you of anything?

In the face of this schism, Augustine confronted a genuine problem, one that is still relevant today. Must we be tolerant of those who are enemies of tolerance? And what price should we pay in order to achieve the necessary unity of the church? Only the saint's final postion is remembered now, but at the beginning he tried to establish a dialogue with the schismatics, to organize public debates, and to negotiate compromises. At last, confronted with the terror the Donatists were inflicting on the population, he decided to counter it by relying on imperial terror. For in the meantime the empire, the temporal power, had become linked to the church, the spiritual power.

Terror against terror—the same fatal spiral of interaction has continued through the centuries. Struggling against the alienation of the people by extremists, Augustine came to justify what soon became the alienation of the same people by the imperial authority. The repression was terrible, and afterwards he tried to moderate it, but he made the mistake of forgetting that in addition to the ecclesial problem—which couldn't be decided by force, anyway—there also existed a genuine political, economic, and social problem. While crying out for the "purification" of religion, the Donatists were also protesting against excessive wealth, and were defending the wretched, exploited, agricultural Berbers against the rich Roman colonists.

This injustice poisoned the religious conflict—is the situation altogether different in the Algeria of today?—and caused it to explode. The church did not bother with such nuances and allied itself completely with the secular authority. It was a harmful alliance, because the theory of "just persecution" developed by Augustine on this occasion was used later, especially during the Middle Ages, to justify every excess committed in the name of church unity. It was a deviation that radically contradicted the spirit of nonviolence, and resulted in the horror we know as the Inquisition. And I must confess, friends in Partenia, that to be named bishop in an area where values so fundamental, in my view, once foundered does not leave me indifferent.

Christian Partenia's real existence was subsequently swallowed up by the Arab invasion of the seventh century and the massive Islamization of the North African territories. Since then, from a Christian point of view, nothing has changed, except that, in the Vatican files, the lost diocese is still listed among the fictive properties for which a titular bishop is responsible.

History sometimes winks: One of my predecessors at Évreux, Bishop Caillot, intervened only once during the proceedings of Vatican II: to ask Rome to suppress these hollow affectations. As we see, he was not heard.

Here I am, then, bishop *in partibus infidelium*, in the land of infidels. I beg you to overlook this unfortunate definition. It belongs to the mentality of another age, one in keeping with the Crusades. Some insolent people, however, maintain that it is quite in keeping with the reproaches that have been made against me.

3

Friday the thirteenth, rue Saint-Louis

DEAR FRIENDS, DO YOU KNOW how one changes from being a resident bishop to being a transferred bishop? Nothing is simpler. Twenty-four hours were enough for me. Plus a few stormy weeks.

Thursday, January 12, 1995: Rome has always thought of me as alone. I was indeed alone at the Congregation, where I appeared before the three prelate-judges. No lawyer. I was alone confronting the hostile dossiers piled up on the desk. A little later when the verdict came down I was still more alone.

Friday, January 13: return to Évreux. People surround the loner from Rome; it's an encouraging crowd. I am treated with great care; some try to console me. I haven't walked under a ladder, but under the Caudine Forks of the Vatican. Apparently, the consequences of the latter are more serious.

It's like the beginning of a wake. Visitors are still in shock, as if they've just learned of a sudden death, with an obituary broadcast on all the television channels. They enter the hall of the bishop's residence on tiptoe, wander around in silence, or whisper in a low voice. People embrace me with tears in their eyes; they don't know what to say. That makes it even worse. I feel as if I'm at my own burial. In this case, however, the dead man, who is alive and in good health, is cheering up the mourners.

That's how Rome wanted it all to end, in despondent intimacy. But does Rome know? The world has changed. The news begins to ring out, and reporters flow through the bishop's residence. The news doesn't have the feeling of mourning and time limits. Two opposed worlds cross each other over a few square yards without colliding.

And then everything gets mixed up. Reinforcements arrive from outside. A protest movement begins to take on serious dimensions. Consternation is followed by mobilization; apathy is replaced by an appetite for life. The bishop's house begins to vibrate, like a mechanism that has been rewound.

For twelve years, 35 rue Saint-Louis was hardly very well behaved behind its long bourgeois façade. It was there, at its heavy sculptured portal, that reverberations of my stormy career ran aground. In itself the residence is hardly exceptional. It is a quiet house, of the kind found in every provincial city, with shining parquet floors smelling of wax, thick walls that retain the summer coolness, and grounds that are crowned with century-old trees. It's a house where one can live apart, and for some time it had already lost its sleepy vocation. After each heavy wind of the Gaillot years, the old residence perked up with visitors, messages, and preparations for the storm. The postman—whom many of my correspondents pitied—brought heavy sacks of mail, without any distinction between messages of praise and attacks. I was the only one who felt that some were heavy and others light.

Friends called, some who were famous—Ibrahim Souss, Sister Emmanuelle, President Aristide—as well as some who were unknown. And then there were the travelers in the night whose problems had to be resolved, though sometimes they were insoluble: nameless people in distress, immigrants on the run, political refugees, those without identity cards, the appallingly destitute, and lonely people knocking on the door at all hours, asking for help if not for the right of asylum, kept the six rooms on the second floor constantly filled.

But the seismic shock in the bishop's residence today is on a different scale. All the TV stations want something live at the same time, the radio stations are looking for a scoop, photographers are hoping for exclusive shots. It's rather amusing when you think about it: by condemning me, those who accuse me of making too many appearances on TV, and talking too much, have helped me beat all records for reaching a large audience. And this time without my having anything to do with it.

No room in the house escapes the whirlwind. Only the little chapel, which was to be my sole refuge during the ensuing days, manages to avoid intrusion. We are grabbed, pushed about, overwhelmed—completely swamped. Telephone, fax, microphone, TV, interview, photograph: these are the only words we hear. The bishop's residence reels like an unsteady ship, yet everything somehow gets organized. It's a crazy atmosphere.

Outside the residence there flash, over and over, signals of a message that has been liberated. On Sunday the fifteenth, in answer to an appeal from the deacons, five thousand people assemble in front of the cathedral. Strictly speaking, it's not a demonstration; it's an outburst, a desire of people to be together, to prove that they exist. For a few instants the bishop's residence is vacant and I am alone; then shouting draws me outside and I realize that rue Saint-Louis is overflowing with a good-natured crowd. I go to meet the crowd. It is a spontaneous meeting—intense moments.

In my office on the first floor, boxes pile up with thousands of letters from all over the world. The switchboard is saturated; the fax machine gives out. Rather than a knockout blow, the Roman bludgeon has delivered a wake-up call. In the future, all these people, all these comrades, who yesterday seemed completely annihilated, from now on would demand ten times more energy from me. They struggle and debate; they assemble, draw up petitions, and take action. Stunned at first, I begin to respond

This ferment will last until Sunday, January 22, the day of my farewell mass for the Diocese of Eure.[2] The cathedral is jammed; thousands of the faithful, from all corners of France, Germany, and Belgium, assemble on the square that is swept by wind and rain. They are the proof, I tell them, "that this sanction has provoked an extraordinary shock wave. From now on, whether in church or society, decisions and choices can no longer be made without taking you into account."

Once again, as in the aftermath of my dismissal, I insist that those moments of great emotion and communion should be understood as an occasion of hope, not a burial service. Perhaps it is also the beginning of great things for those who struggle for a church open to the world. I do not forget them in my homily:

> We are assembled here to open the book of Life. The word of God is our light for the road ahead of us. It is a Word that heals and liberates the hearts of those who are wounded.
>
> Let there be no hate, no violence in us.
>
> Our hearts are not made to hate.
>
> An earthquake in Japan, men tearing each other to pieces in Chechyna, young people without jobs

2. The town of Évreux is located in the French department (or administrative state) of Eure. Gaillot refers to his diocese sometimes by the town name and sometimes by the departmental location.

wandering in the wild nights of the suburbs—all these things are enough to distress God.

Nevertheless, do not weep. Don't go into mourning. This is a holiday, a day of rejoicing.

The wave of confidence and solidarity that has suddenly spread among such diverse people has become a rumor of hope.

The event that has taken place is a revelation of deep unfulfilled aspirations both in society and the church: the aspiration for freedom of speech, the right to be different, respect for every man and woman's dignity, for democracy. These are values that many claim and are still waiting for, since, very often, those in authority act and decide without taking people into account.

The headlines read, "For the bishop of Évreux, the mass is over." But I solemnly declare that what has happened will not make me stop:

What I have experienced with you here in this diocese of Évreux, what I have experienced elsewhere in all kinds of circumstances and occasions, shows me clearly that the words of Christ are the only path of Mission to take, and that every Christian, every community, every church that does not, before everything else, take the path of those in distress has no chance to be heard as a bearer of the Good News.

Everyone, every community, and every church that does not, first and above all, express its solidarity with every man and woman will be unable to find the path of his or her heart, the secret place where this Good News can be received.

> For my part, in communion with the church, I will
> continue along my path in order to bring the Good
> News to the poor. . . .

Dear friends in Partenia, that is how the events ended
that bring me among you today—in a kind of renewing
fever, a kind of apotheosis of solidarity, on rue Saint-Louis,
the very place it all began twelve years ago.

DURING THAT TIME, people very far from Évreux at first
judged this outpouring of support with disdain. In spite of
successive warnings, the signals that shifted to red, they
hoped—to use a sports term—to play for time. In ousting
me, they did not believe at first that they were unleashing a
vast movement of protest among the faithful. Then, too, they
counted on it rapidly running out of steam. Some had even
openly stated that the reactions and protests had been
"blown up" by the press, that the fever was stronger in micro-
phones than in the street, that journalists had entered into
conspiracies on my behalf, and there had been a "disinfor-
mation" campaign conducted by professionals. It is always
the same trial of media witchcraft. More than two weeks
after my transfer, Rome still hadn't heard the voices that
were calling out from all over France and other European
countries. Apparently it's still difficult for sound to pass
through the walls of infallibility.

But rue Saint-Louis did not grow weary. The blow, so
brutally inflicted, has not fallen again.

4 ～

The satanic mass media

As you know, my friends, I am often criticized for exposing the bishop's image to the media firing line, of appearing too frequently on TV, of getting lost under the bright lights of stardom. Sometimes the accusations even sound like an indictment. The grand inquisitors of public opinion point to "satanic broadcasts," libertine magazines, and irreligious papers; because I dare to appear in them, they consider me as a source of scandal, someone who is destroying the faith.

The substance of what I say is of little importance to them. My accusers seem indifferent to the care I take never to betray at any time, regardless of the place, the circumstances, or the occcasion, the profound meaning of my mission. It doesn't matter to them that I bring God's word to the widest possible audience. Meticulous and frozen censors, my critics stigmatize the set design of variety talk shows, angrily denounce my presence in such dens of iniquity, and rage against the priest who wears a small cross on his lapel and is not afraid of "bad company." I have always been struck by the hullabaloo caused by my television appearances. With very rare exceptions—-the conversation with Drewermann,[3] for example—criticism of the offending show deals only with form, style, the genre, and other characteristics that escape me. Little is made of the substance of the message that I try to get across. To me, however, that hardly seems unimportant. When they see me scribbling, rather awkwardly, on the blackboard used in one of these shows, some good people who have strong traditionalist inclinations cover their eyes and cry out against scandal. It matters little to them that millions of people watching television are watching me draw an Easter sun, a message of faith and hope. A bishop who sketches, that's not respectable . . .

When they see me laugh on entertainment shows—which generally reach far larger audiences than church-sponsored programs such as "The Lord's Day"—they cry heresy. As if a bishop should not respond to humor, and it was forbidden for him to share in the merriment of ordinary people.

---

3. Eugen Drewermann, a prolific and controversial German Catholic theologian.

Why shouldn't he have the right to say what he has to say on such a stage? Are there any arenas forbidden to the Gospel?

In 1988 I responded favorably to a journalist at *Gai-Pied* who asked me for an article on the theme, "To be a Catholic and a homosexual today." I wasn't familiar with the magazine, but it didn't matter. I sent him a text. I'm going to let you in on a secret: the *same* article (yes, the very same text!) had been published in *La Croix*[4] the previous week—only the layout had changed. But its appearance in *Gai-Pied* was a scandal. As if the word of Christ, the word of tolerance and acceptance—as if the Good News, the message of fraternity—was meant only for certain groups.

I realize that appearing on forbidden pages did me a great deal of harm in high Roman circles. Father Calvet, a hyper-traditionalist monk from the monastery of Barroux, helped *Gai-Pied*'s sales considerably when he distributed several copies in the offices of the Curia on September 28, 1990.

But the church has entered with me in the publications in which I have appeared. I have managed to start a dialogue in unusual places. Is the priest who opened a small restaurant in the notorious Pigalle district of Paris doing anything different? His "priest's café," wedged between two sex-shops, is an oasis of fraternity in that spiritual and emo-

---

4. The highly respected and widely circulated French Catholic daily newspaper.

tional wasteland more desolate than the desert that today covers Partenia. That priest in Pigalle does not force people to pray—but there is a chapel above the café.

Everyone agrees that the Gospel should be proclaimed to all people and to all nations. But when it's a question of being commited to this position, that's another story.

What are we afraid of?

THE CHURCH SPEAKS constantly of "responding to the challenge of the media," but these words are not put into practice. The institution remains obstinately suspicious of "opinion makers," and presents only a fleeting profile as soon as it feels beset by the press. Is it a sign of openness, for example, that people see us shut in at Lourdes every year for the episcopal conference, with debates held only behind closed doors? By remaining constantly on guard, and being suspicious of everything not dependent on it, of everything that does not move within its immediate circle, the church ends up losing contact with the world of communication—and with the world as a whole. When presented to the outside, the church no longer controls its subject, and no longer has secure landmarks at its disposal. Rather than feel less powerful, it gives up trying to explain itself or make itself understood, and gets entangled in a sterile cycle: it fears what it does not know, and ignores what it does not want to know.

There is nothing very new in this attitude of withdrawal. For a long time, the church has supped at the table of the media-devil with a long spoon. The problem is that today everyone goes on feasting without it. And without place servings. Once this reality is recognized, there are two possible attitudes: either the church continues to shut itself off in its splendid isolation—ignoring the times, concentrating fervently on putting out parish bulletins, and forgetting that life unfolds outside without it—or it genuinely opens itself up to the modern world, and exploits (in the best sense of the word) every possibility of involvement in the life of today.

The dilemma is always the same: either remain in the cathedral or venture out onto the street. Consistent with myself, I made my choice: I go to the media in order to meet others, to reach those whom the church no longer touches, to bring the church out of its ghetto and help it take its proper place among all the factors in people's growth. It would be wonderful if other bishops—not always the same ones— would also express themselves in the media. Let there be many of them and let them speak often. If a representative of the church interests the media, it means that the church is still interesting. We should rejoice at this rather than become alarmed. I try to offer the image of a tolerant and receptive church open to dialogue with modernity. Society is questioning itself. What harm is there in attempting to bring it some elements of a response?

I am not sure, friends in Partenia, that you completely understand what the problem is. Media madness probably does not reach your mountains very often. I can already hear my detractors making fun of me, and pretending to pity me: "How will he be able to stand the lack of attention? He'll have withdrawal pains, he's so overdosed on TV!" Let their minds be at ease. This detoxification will perhaps be good for me.

Besides, I don't run after the media; I never ask to be interviewed or to appear on a program. I am invited, and sometimes I accept; it's that simple.

This is not without risks or a few small hitches. I am not sure if I always manage to emerge intact from that jungle of images and soundwaves which in many ways is both dizzying and smothering. Once you have entered the heart of the media monster, you are inevitably confronted with certain excesses and lapses which, without being your direct responsibility, strike you by ricochet. I often say that it's easier for me to preach in the cathedral than to find myself in a television studio where I'm not in control—far from it. I do not control the questions or the amount of time I can speak, much less the technical aspects of the program, like its editing. Is that a reason for not jumping into the arena? After all, what are we afraid of? A trap? People often say that: "Gaillot has been trapped again." This annoys me a great deal. Frankly, I don't feel that journalists generally are trying to trap me. On the contrary, I have found many of them listen well and I have learned a great deal through my contacts with them. I don't pretend to agree with all their interpretations. But that's the nature of the genre.

AGAIN, WHAT ARE WE AFRAID OF? Of not presenting a perfect image? Of being taken out of context, challenged, and even pilloried? "I have been sent to bring the Good News to the ends of the earth," said Paul, the apostle to the nations. We ought to be apostles who follow in Paul's path. Jesus gave his very life in order that the Word might be able to reach pagans. To reach the others, all the others, we too must be capable of always giving more, of offering ourselves without receiving something in return, while accepting the fact that we will be seasoned with every sauce—and some are more bitter than sweet. We are not building the church for ourselves, but for others. And in any case, the media are the most remarkable means of communication that we have at our disposal. Above all, we need to abandon the illusion that we can totally control media representatives who invite our participation. If they welcome us on their programs, so much the better; let us allow ourselves to be welcomed without prejudice or preconditions. Gabriel Ringlet, vice-rector of the University of Louvain and a specialist in communication, warns us, "Going on television calls for a great deal of self-surrender."

The important thing is to be honest, to give expression to what inspires us. And above all, to carry the Word as far as possible.

5

The extended family

DEAR FRIENDS IN PARTENIA, one day or another they will speak to you about me in a mysterious tone. It's better to anticipate them. Some day, they will tell you: "Jacques Gaillot has had two lives. First, that of a priest, with no special history, someone living in the bosom of the church. A smooth journey, without the slightest jolt. And then, without anyone really knowing why, he changes direction, and heads into the high winds."

If they are well informed, they will provide you with a few details: "In the parish at Saint-Dizier (about 100 miles west of Paris), he was also professor at the major seminary of Châlons; then he was at (the nearby city of) Reims,

48

where a little later he became director of the seminary. Charged next with the permanent training of priests at the liturgical institute, he was named vicar-general of the Diocese of Langres (fifty miles southeast of Saint-Dizier). Still no complaints about him: Gaillot always sang in the midst of the church without the least false note. Apart from the circle of the initiated, no one ever heard his voice, no one knew him. Neither in the Diocese of Eure, where he was named bishop in 1982 at the age of 46, or anywhere else. It was there at Évreux that the second birth of Jacques Gaillot took place."

This "second birth"—which rejuvenated me considerably, and is not so disagreeable—has intrigued everyone. People would like to have a rational explanation for it, to be able to follow its stages and understand its progression. They would also like to uncover some secret: I am suspected of having hidden my intentions, of having champed at the bit, of having known how to keep silent for years—and who knows what else?

My answer is more simple, and my personality a good deal less cunning. I was not programmed—either to become bishop of Évreux, or to say what I say, or to do what I do. And I'm still not. When I arrived at Évreux, I didn't know that life was going to shake me up. In simple terms, I just act according to the dictates of my heart and my convictions, guided by the Gospel. And I go where people and events call me. Is that so unlikely and so hard to understand?

If I may say so, one event alone changed everything. Beginning in 1982, I became a dignitary of the church. But if certain events were especially significant—if becoming a bishop opened up new horizons to me—I know that what drives me today has always been a part of me.

On June 20, 1982, in the cathedral of Évreux, I received the crosier, the miter, and the ring. A number of Christians from the Haute-Marne made the trip and introduced me to the members of the Diocese of Eure. A group of people who had given me their support entrusted me to another community.

Their remarks were forceful:

"We know Gaillot. You'll see, he's a high-speed train."

Since then, there has been a wealth of images used to describe me: from "an off-road vehicle," and "a four-wheeler of religion," to the decoder of "the scrambled church."

At the microphone a worker from Langres explained:

"Residents of the Diocese of Eure, your tranquility is over. . . . One evening, Father Gaillot paid me a visit, as he did to other members of the parish team. He came to ask me if, eventually, I would agree to be a deacon, but my wife had to give her consent to it. Nothing more nor less. At that moment, if a bomb had fallen on a corner of the house, it wouldn't have had more of an effect. My reply was the same as that of the others who had been asked: Why me? . . . But Father Gaillot was so persuasive, so convincing, that we agreed to try the adventure with him. During the years of our journey toward the diaconate, he was present at all the meetings, enlightening us, guiding us in our training, going over each stage with us. We are sometimes told that Jesus Christ challenges us, causes us trouble, upsets our whole life. Well, as I turn to you, members of the Diocese of Évreux, I tell you: Your tranquility is over, Father Gaillot is going to disturb you. If you are asleep, Father Gaillot is going to wake you up. He's going to knock on your door, and like us, you're going to say, 'Come in.' Then you too will be caught, hooked, you'll have to say 'yes.'"

I had to share with you that warning from my friend from Haut-Marne because, to be truthful, I haven't changed much between Langres and Partenia. And I might as well admit it to you: I fully intend to remain always open to the unpredictable, to the signs that God may wish to place on my path.

"It is up to us to keep going"

AT ÉVREUX, AFTER MY EXPERIENCE at Langres, I gave offense again. Jesus spent his life awakening our freedoms. That also seems our role. All during the twelve years I spent there, and by every means at my disposal, I tried to make sure that ordinary people got a hearing, to awaken consciences, to reveal individuals to themselves and others. Sometimes through an increased presence; sometimes, in contrast, by making myself as inobtrusive as possible, and not allowing my influence to be felt on the issues and choices that were being debated, particularly during the diocesan synod, which went on for three years, from 1988 to 1991. With increasing freedom of action and expression, both clergy and laity began to take on greater responsibilities. Little by little this new alliance took over the diocese. Everywhere, active communities were created in parishes that formed groups for the preparation for baptism and marriage, coordinated the training of catechists, handled finances, and dealt with elected officials.

New initiatives were begun:

From one neighborhood to the next, Workshops of Solidarity, the brainchild of a deacon, began to carry out a regular spider's web of small jobs.

In Networks of Mutuality, everyone exchanged his or her special competence: cooking, helping with math homework, reading, masonry, sewing.

The Myosotis Association, which was directed by lay people, acquired a lodge opposite the prison. It became a genuine haven of peace and support for the relatives of prisoners. Children are entertained there while their mother is in the visiting room; a father or a fiancée is comforted after an especially difficult visit; sometimes it's simply a matter of sharing a cup of cocoa. Previously, families had to wait on the sidewalk, enduring the sometimes embarrassing glances from curious passers-by in a small town.

Under the leadership of Anne-Marie, a woman religious, the solidarity committee took on such actions as sheltering a young girl who was in danger, giving the right of asylum to an immigrant, looking for shelter for a homeless family, and accompanying individuals to governmental agencies. This committee also gave birth to the Pause Café, a place for listening and rehabilitation. "Rehabilitation," a former prisoner explains, "cannot come from outside forces; we ourselves have to achieve it. But we need to talk, to have someone to confide in. That's why we created the Pause Café."

Friends in Partenia, I suspect you haven't heard about all these everyday activities, this concern for people, carried on by the Christians of the diocese. You were too far from Évreux.

IT WAS EQUALLY IMPORTANT, however, that this energetic and active church speak out openly. That it express itself not only on problems that directly involve the local church but also on the broader questions of life and its conflicts. "When you speak up," I used to say to my parishioners, "I will be silent." At first that made them laugh. They did not have enough confidence in themselves, or else not enough in me. Finally, they came to realize that it was possible—even if it wasn't always simple.

Let me give a few examples. A truck farmer had killed some thieves. It seemed to us that he thought his action was justifiable self-defense. But many Christians in the group wanted to respond, or at least to raise the issue for discussion: Should a person take justice into one's own hands? Are a few carrots worth a human life? Because of the unpopularity of this position, however, they were afraid to speak up in front of the others about the matter.

Something similar took place when local politicians tried to eliminate the allocations "for families of immigrants suspected of delinquency." Christians in our diocese were divided: The proposal seemed unjust to some, but most of them felt that the decision should be left to the politicians, and that those living in the housing projects would probably not accept the word of the church in this period of economic crisis anyway. Finally, however, some lay people drew up a statement, a very prudent declaration. It was issued only after I had expressed myself, since local journalists, astonished at the silence of the church of Évreux when faced with an issue dealing with human rights, had questioned me.

After the murder of a young woman and the unrelated establishment, amidst lots of commotion, of a community of Jehovah's Witnesses—two events which, on different levels, aroused a great deal of emotion in the area—the pastoral council asked me to intervene. "You are the church—speak; I will express myself afterwards," I told them. And that is what they did. I was very happy about this; one is never disappointed when Christians speak out.

I WANTED TO PROTECT this freedom of expression and initiative, right to the end. Perhaps that is why several members of my diocese were astonished at my docility towards Cardinal Gantin. They felt that I had accepted the situation too readily.

I replied that I wanted neither to justify myself nor to avoid punishment: To defend myself at every step, and then try to keep my position, would not have helped anyone, especially not the Christians of Eure, who I felt were ready to get into a wrestling match with Rome. I did not want to take part in any action, and I let the associations and groups organize without me. It was not my place to act; it was up to them to follow their conscience. I didn't want my presence, or a phrase from me, to influence their decisions. During the days that followed my eviction, I may have disappointed some who were close to me; I let myself get taken over by journalists, and some long-time companions got tired of waiting for me. They wanted to hear my point of view on what strategy to adopt, whereas I was confident that even in that disorderly hullaballoo they were capable of guaranteeing both the present and the future—of the Church of Évreux, not of Jacques Gaillot.

And today I am happy to hear them say, in the name of solidarity, fraternity, and love, "It's up to us to continue what Jacques began."

In fact, the Christians of Eure continue to place their trust in the principal decisions taken during our synod:

> In fidelity to the Gospel, the diocesan church, at every level, affirms its option for the poor and the outcast, both in France and in the third world. Every disciple of Jesus Christ should wage this battle for the dignity of human beings, for truth and justice in the distribution of goods and wealth.

For its part, the Church of Évreux commits itself to make this option visible:

- in its ministries, the representatives it chooses, and the responsibilities entrusted to lay people;

- in its financial decisions;

- in the lifestyles of its communities;

- by favoring the participation of the outcasts themselves in the development of projects that concern them.

6

"The score is wonderful, but the orchestra plays off-key"

WHEN I SAY THAT I AM GOING to Partenia alone, stripped of my office, excluded from my official functions by the Roman referees, I am forgetting the priests and deacons who volunteered to accompany me, and the Christians who decided that in the future they would send the whole of their church offering to my new diocese. And I am forgetting the commotion in the background, the enormous murmur of protest that arose from the sanctions against me. Let it be clearly understood that I never wanted the incident to be reduced to

57

me. It is not my person that is at stake. We must go beyond the case of the bishop of Évreux; we must not become polarized over his removal.

My personal problem hardly matters. What is important is elsewhere. It is to be found among those thousands of people whom some have wished to humiliate through me, and who today still hold themselves erect. In spite of the blows they have received, in spite of their sufferings, these voiceless men and women—who have so often been evoked by Abbé Pierre—are making themselves heard en masse. Too long ignored, misunderstood, or scorned, and previously considered as negligible in number, they explode because of "the Gaillot affair." It's the classic story of the drop of water. They consider that, this time, the church has gone too far in ignoring the aspirations of part of its people, and that it should no longer act as if it were the proprietor of God, Christ, and the Gospel.

These people are not all unconditional supporters— "Gaillolators," according to a recently coined expression. Far from it, which is all to the good. The messages of support and testimonies of solidarity sometimes included criticisms or reservations about certain forms my action took. But the Vatican tempest swept aside our minor disagreements. This was the case for the Christians of Eure, who felt humiliated at seeing their bishop sacked without the least consultation with the most active members of the diocese. The same thing is true of all those Christians who protest today. They no longer wish to be taken for children to whom one would say, "You have made mistake; don't try to understand, just obey." They are adults, and no longer accept truths that are handed down from on high. They reflect, they feel the need to be informed, they demand the right to speak freely. And they are told: "You don't count."

The Vatican can accuse me of many mistakes, accumulate criticisms, and pronounce sentence, but it cannot ignore, much less deny, the birth of a public opinion in the church. It made its appearance apparently in order to defend me, to show that I was not alone among Christian people, but beyond that and even more profoundly, to call for a church of freedom where people would be able to have a dialogue without condemning each other, a church with a courage that could be lived within an evangelical dynamic.

I have been criticized for, among other things, "keeping too much distance" from the institution and the bishops. I have not dug any ditch, but at the same time I have refused to remain fixed in place, hiding behind the august character of my office. I descended into the arena. If wanting to become aware of the realities of everyday life, of the problems of ordinary people, their sufferings, desires, and needs, wherever they are and whatever their religious attitudes, means "keeping too much distance" from the church, I plead guilty. If, in order to get closer to the outcast and those brutalized by society, to extend my hand to those who most need it, to mix with prisoners and those on the verge of despair, to seek out those who have been made to feel unwelcome in the church, I have had to place myself on the other side, I plead guilty.

But doesn't the real distance that has been underlined lie elsewhere? Isn't it the one that increasingly separates an Ice Age church, cold and authoritarian, walled up within its certitudes, and a Christian people who have had enough of a confiscated Word and a stifled freedom? The people who today protest openly call for a church that would be more human and more involved with its times. Isn't the real distance that between a discourse that clings to outmoded morality and believers who no longer listen to it? Isn't the real distance one that cuts us off from our own people?

The church reacts as if it had everything to fear from a debate within itself, from a contested dialogue with its faithful. At Évreux, in our episcopal team, there was always debate. Synods were held in local churches, religious and laity inaugurated projects together, accepted active responsibilities, and participated in decisions that involved the future of the diocese. Votes were taken at the end to conclude the discussions. How can one believe that this heartbeat of the rank-and-file, which allows everyone to move forward, should not find an echo at the church's summit? Up there, however, if an opinion does not agree with the party line, it is not considered. Instead, they issue orders and demand blind obedience. "The Catholic hierarchy," Robert Solé writes in *Le Monde*, "is perceived as an organized bloc, with its assemblies, commissions, and spokesmen. On anything important, there is no pluralism worth mentioning." One must march in step.

Are they right, those who claim that "religions are allergic to discussion"?

It is not a question, moreover, of jeopardizing the foundations of the edifice. All the faithful who struggle in their aspiration for greater liberty retain their respect for an institution they wouldn't dream of rejecting. As for myself, as my judges readily conceded, I have never been suspected of mistreating dogma. I don't think I ever failed in my apostolic mission, or sent out a message that was contrary to my apostolate. I have never wanted a rupture, or a break with the church. My place is in the church; it is my family, and I will continue to serve it with all my strength. It is through the church that I discovered the Gospel and the way of fraternity. I am not making myself a leader of some dissident position. To my opponents, to those who sometimes accuse me of preaching a different church, I simply say they are mistaken: I preach a church that is different.

Must we accept that the church should behave as if time has stopped, as if it had nothing to learn or gain from the evolution of our society?

In truth, this is an untenable position: The church will not be able to maintain its opposition to change much longer, unless one wants to accept its steadily increasing distance from our society, and become resigned to see it, cemented into its past, take refuge on a small island.

Thousands of Christians reject such an alternative. That is why they rush into the breach opened up by the Gaillot affair.

My Final Rudeness

FRIENDS OF PARTENIA, you will surely have been made to understand that you have inherited a bishop who has no manners. I speak when I should keep quiet and, what is more, on problems that do not directly concern me. I am a brainless pawn because, as a priest, I don't have to worry about what everyone else is discussing. (For example, AIDS: Should I pretend I don't know anything about it?) Instead, I answer questions which I shouldn't even be asked and what is more, without taking offense or paying much attention to the locale of the interview, or what kind of a show I'm appearing on. I irritate people when I try to be simple, I manage to shock when I am sincere, I am a source of extra annoyance when I go out in the open. Above all, I forget to let people know what I'm doing ahead of time.

Don't smile, friends of Partenia. It must all seem rather strange to you, but even if it is likely that I have been sacrificed at the altar of an ecclesiastical unity demanded at any price, it is not impossible that my bad manners had something to do with it.

"Of course," Archbishop Jean-Louis Tauran asked me, during the January 12 session of the Vatican tribunal, "you called on the bishops of Haiti?"

I had just returned from Haiti. During a very brief visit to that country, I had filmed a television program for

France 2 on the condition of children in Haiti. But in Rome they didn't ask me about the distressing condition of those children; they were concerned about protocol. No, I had not met the bishops. I had written to them, but clearly, that wasn't enough.

It was my last demonstration of rudeness as bishop of Évreux, my final breach of manners. Is it really so important? Must there be a reserved area, a private enclosure, for a bishop? Doesn't he participate in the universal mission? Is he not to act wherever he finds himself, wherever a crisis requires him to? Must he wait for a green light from the institution, a safe-conduct pass, an authorization to travel? What reality do diocesan boundaries correspond to in these final years of the twentieth century? What meaning do they have when the world has shrunk to the point where all parts of it are within the easy reach of voices and images?

I am not class conscious nor do I have the instinct of proprietorship; I did not protest when Cardinal Gantin came to the department of Eure on several occasions without alerting me, as bishop of the area. I was unwelcome, it seems, at the golden anniversary of the ordination of his friend Father Raymond Naguet, nor was I invited to the religious professions that took place in December 1993 under his presidency at the abbey of Bec-Hellouin. Was I upset? Certainly not. Except that today I am forced to wonder whether, by visiting exclusively the anti-Gaillot faction of the Diocese of Eure, the cardinal didn't inevitably run the risk of hearing only one side?

My brother bishops were always welcome in my diocese, even without going through the customary formalities. Today Partenia is open to them. They should consider themselves invited whether they inform me of their visit in advance or not.

A solo bishop?

BISHOP OF PARTENIA IN ALGERIA, I remain a member of the episcopal conference of the Church of France. This is a rather incongruous situation, you say, but after all, the link with my peers remains, and that's the important thing. I have often been accused of subjecting this link to intolerable distortions. According to them, I acted like the Lone Ranger to the point of cutting into episcopal solidarity. But should one really hide behind a purely external unity, keeping silent because others don't speak out? Must a bishop's voice necessarily be his master's voice? It should not be judged discordant simply because it does not agree with others in every respect. Why should we all have to be built on the same model, feel the same emotions, the same sense of outrage at the same time? Are we robots, beings with programmed, inevitably collective sensibility directed by remote control? Cardinal Joseph Ratzinger, prefect of the Congregation for Faith and Doctrine and hardly to be suspected of excessive liberalism, himself admits, in an interview in the Catholic journal *La Vie*, that "the existence of different currents of thought seems necessary if an excessive conformism is to be avoided. . . . The Christian message is universal. It addresses itself, therefore, to very different people. It is to be expected that there would be diverse approaches: Recall the differences between St. Paul and St. Peter, St. John and St. Mark. It is natural for the Church to make use of different forms of expression which, of course, grow out of the freedom of expression of persons and groups. The universality of the Church, therefore, implies plurality. Otherwise, the Church would not be universal."

If a bishop wants to communicate, to participate in the society's debates, he cannot at the same time observe delays that were appropriate in the last century. When journalists stick a microphone under your nose and cameras are trained on you, should you, if you think you would be performing a useful service by expressing yourself, nevertheless lower the curtain and wait for a painfully drawn up common statement, which won't be issued by the appropriate commission for several weeks? Cooled off, lost in the flood of constantly breaking headlines, it would no longer interest anyone. Should we behave as though we were in the army and admit that, as regards the institution and the Vatican, a bishop can be nothing but a soldier sworn to blind obedience? Is a bishop so unworthy of confidence that he is never to take the initiative in making a statement apart from group announcements?

I recall the interrogation of one of my correspondents: "What should unity within the church and the solidarity of bishops be like? Should it follow the example of the great

Stalinist rallies of former days, offering a terrifying vision of an anonymous crowd whose thought had been poured into an iron discipline? Or, on the contrary, should there be the possibility to debate, to discuss, to advance togther while safeguarding one's personality, one's originality, one's way of bearing witness to the Gospel?"

I believed in the second possibility. To remind me of my "duties," people have constantly quoted the fraternal counsel—presented as a severe warning in the Vatican communiqué—that the pope gave me during an *ad limina* visit in 1992: "It's not enough to sing outside the choir; one must also sing with the others." But does that mean that within the church people are no longer to be themselves?

I remain in communion with the bishops as a whole, united around the successor of Peter. But why reject freedom of expression within the institution, and especially on the problems of society? Unity is not achieved by having all the bishops say the same thing about everything, in the same style and at the same time. Unity does not mean: "I want to see only one miter!" Such an authoritarian process does not present the visage of evangelical freedom.

I am not going to play the little game of "It's not me, it's the other person." That would be ridiculous and a little late. But when I've been rapped on the knuckles at episcopal assemblies for "an improper attitude for a bishop" (to use the expression of one journalist), I found myself all alone. So much for episcopal solidarity.

In April 1994, when I received a warning from Archbishop Duval, I didn't receive a single fraternal letter, one message of support from a bishop. Where was this solidarity that is extolled so highly in the church? That silence was a signal of marginalization.

For some time I appeared to be the black sheep of the episcopacy, someone who systematically challenged everything, who did the opposite of what the pope suggested, and played a solo role.

This was true in appearances, but a little less so behind the scenes. As proof of this I offer several examples.

If we dared to speak about our doubts

• My involvement with the Palestinian drama in the territories occupied by Israel shocked public opinion, just as did my meeting with Arafat. Five years later, the pope received the leader of the PLO as a head of state, and Israel recognized him as negotiator in a peace process that had been very difficult to launch.

• When I mentioned the suffering of divorced and remarried Catholics who are excluded from the Eucharist, I wasn't introducing anything new; I was simply saying out loud what many others thought. The bishops of northern France, among whom I was included, had asked Rome on several occasions for a modification of this rule.

• The same thing is true concerning the use of contraceptives as part of the fight against AIDS. This time I quote from the commentary of Serge Lafitte, a journalist with *L'Actualité religieuse:*[5]

> For the church, the prohibition of contraceptives does not allow any exceptions. At least that is the official version. Nevertheless, other bishops have indicated a position on this subject very close to their disturbing confrère, but too often, in such a roundabout manner, without even pronouncing the controversial word, that people are genuinely unsure whether they have affirmed what they have seemed to say.

In other words, the important thing is the letter, not the spirit. And that's hardly a problem that just began now.

• In 1984 seven bishops voted against the text, "Achieving Peace," which had been adopted by the episcopal assembly at Lourdes. The session took place behind closed doors, but journalists contacted several prelates who were undoubtedly suspected of this electoral mutiny. *Liberation*[6] called me. I answered, making the point that this text gave legitimacy to nuclear weapons. The other opponents of the document preferred to abstain from all commentary. It was their right to be silent; it was my right to speak.

• In October 1988, again at Lourdes, I wanted to debate the questions of married priests and the ordination of married men. I mentioned my uneasiness as a pastor in the

---

5. A distinguished, Catholic-edited, interreligious biweekly.

6. A large-circulation, liberal daily in Paris. (Trans.)

face of the diminishing number of ordinations. It is not the status of the priest that is of crucial importance but the needs of our faith communities. After all, why should we ignore former priests who have married, but remain equipped with precious knowledge and experience? By presenting my questions openly, however, I had again made myself conspicuous. Nevertheless, in the mail that I received subsequently at Évreux, 2,010 letters were favorable to my intervention; 560 came from priests, eleven from bishops.

I have always known that in private several bishops—even while not approving my methods and especially my frequent appearances in the media—were not very far from my position. The only problem is, who could know this if they were prepared to leave their questions unvoiced, while reciting in public, almost word for word, the official language that in secret they were far from completely accepting?

Such an attitude can have serious consequences at a time when, because of fear of the future, both society and the church are beating strategic retreats, while traditionalists, indeed, fundamentalists, are proceeding with vigor. And they know how to make themselves heard.

My dismissal has undoubtedly produced shock waves within the French episcopacy. There are two basic reasons for this. The first is certainly the mobilization of rank-and-file Christians. Their rallies, their activities, and their petitions undoubtedly influenced the bishops' reactions in a significant way. Pressed from all sides by the *vox populi*, the prelates

could no longer continue to remain silent. Another important
element is the awkwardness—and lack of solidarity—shown
them by the Vatican. Most of the bishops learned of my dismissal through the press. It was at once an affront
(Archbishop Duval had pleaded with the Holy See for
patience, but obviously they didn't listen to him) and a new
proof of the existence at the top of a system which has auto-
cratic tendencies and is self-enclosed.

Jean-Pierre Lintanf, a Dominican priest, was quite
explicit in his commentary:[7]

> The process by which the Vatican has removed Bishop
> Gaillot from his charge reveals an extremely danger-
> ous mode of operation in the church. The measures
> taken in this case by Roman authority are brutally in
> opposition to the traditional ecclesiology that had been
> restored to honor and practice by Vatican II, after a
> period of unrestrained and totalitarian centralism. Are
> bishops merely the disposable pawns of an all-powerful
> central administration, prefects who are the delegates
> of a sovereign power that is concentrated in Rome?

From then on, there were two types of reaction that
should be mentioned. The first is compassion, which is the
least one might expect from a Christian bishop. But frankly,
I would have preferred a little less compassion *after* the
event, and a little more solidarity *before*. I believe that if the
bishops had shown some determination, Rome would not

---

7. *Actualité religieuse*, February 15, 1995.

have sacked me. Confronted, if one may say so, with a weak consensus, authority felt it had a free hand.

In addition, there were what I would call "positive reactions," those of bishops who raised real questions. Judged from the outside, their voices might appear timid. But Abbé Pierre reminded us that this challenge to a Roman decision, and the positions that were taken—like the request for the convocation of an extraordinary general assembly of bishops, for example—were to his knowledge a unique event in the church. Nor do I forget the presence of four bishops at Évreux on January 22, or the approach that leaders of the episcopal conference made to the pope.

Some insist, "There you are: in the church everyone has to think alike." For many of us, this boils down to asking us not to think at all. But do they care about what the people of God think? "The score [the Gospel] is wonderful," someone wrote me, "but the orchestra [the church] is off key." To live the Gospel is to be less concerned about disagreements with other bishops or with the institution—especially, I repeat, when they don't threaten communion in the faith— than with trying to live as close as possible to ordinary people, sharing their joys and their hopes, their sorrows and their agonies. A bishop's strength is to be with his people. And the only real censure is that of the people of God. Christian faith does not make us either detached from realities or lost in the clouds. No, Christians walk the roads of history, their foreheads brushing the stars.

7

God, dogma, and society

WHAT HAVE I COME TO DO in your midst, my friends? What role should I adopt, both as a priest and as a bishop?

Sometimes people tell me, "You ought to be the guardian of dogma; you ought to set an example. Instead, you hang out with the world as it is; you run after it and flatter it."

I might as well warn you right away: I will no more act as a guardian in Partenia than I did in Évreux. In the past, to keep me quiet, they sent me back to my vegetable garden and my sacristy; today they draw on dogma. Their argument, however, is taken from the bottom of a trunk that smells of dust.

When he began his public life, Christ chose the most cosmopolitan city:

> He left Nazareth and went to live in Capernaum by the sea near the territory of Zebulum and Naphtali, to fulfill what had been said through Isaiah the prophet:
>
> > "Land of Zebulum, land of Naphtali
> > along the sea beyond the Jordan,
> > heathen Galilee:
> > a people living in darkness
> > has seen a great light.
> > On those who inhabit a land overshadowed by
> > death, light has arisen." (Mt 4:13–16)

For Jesus, the word must ring out in the places where people meet each other. And it seems to me essential for a bishop not to proceed like a demagogue, but to immerse himself in society, while keeping his sights on the Gospel. That's not very easy. As I have already said, I could have spent my time between my office in the bishop's residence and the cathedral, and managed my diocese within the limited horizon of faithful churchgoers, at peace with themselves in their polished shoes. My life would have flowed like a long, tranquil river. But would I have been doing my job as bishop?

We cannot ignore the question of ordinary people without running the risk of becoming completely cut off from reality.

The pope reminds us of the great moral principles; that's his role. But our mission also consists of taking into account the questions and sufferings of those around us.

Despite that, it's not a question of endorsing all of society's bad habits, of clinging to its iniquities, or of opposing everything the church says. But how can we ignore the degree to which the great moral principles can sometimes be inapplicable on the level of everyday life, and the extent to which they prove in some respects to be inhuman?

When so many of our youth have been cut down by illness, when AIDS is spreading with fantastic speed, should we hang on exclusively to an uncompromising discourse that we know is in vain? Should we simply brandish our anathema without concern for cruel reality? I know that the modern era is one of strange combinations and that positions I have taken have frequently been radicalized. An example is my position on condoms. I have never claimed that they were an ideal solution, only an emergency measure. To make abstinence the primary consideration when we are preaching to adolescents is plainly useless. It's simply not being realistic—refusing to see the world as it is. Such an approach suggests that we have never been with young people in their "terminal phase." I am not in favor of using condoms; I am in favor of life.

Life comes ahead of dogmas. Actions are more important than talk. Spirituality is more important than morality. And most of all, the human being takes priority.

The needs of the people, not the rules of the church, come first. The Gospel is where I learned that love is stronger than law.

Jesus performed some miracles on the Sabbath because the needs of the people took precedence over principles. He was reproached for this. In his image, we should adopt every necessary means to save lives, in order to help people hold themselves erect, to respect their dignity and their word. And we will certainly not accomplish that by making them feel guilty and trying to do their thinking for them. God seeks out each individual because each human being is important, and nothing is ever lost.

To condemn someone without appeal is to put the person in the moral position of the recidivist. Acceptance without conditions, without reference to the past, opens up a future. Acceptance does not mean approval, but respect for another person out of concern for tolerance, in order that you may travel part of the road together. It is a road on which that person will, in turn, be invited to fraternity, to listening, and to concern for others.

The church does not exist for itself; that is why it must learn to listen before speaking, as Jesus did on the road to Emmaus, surprising his companions by listening attentively and for a long while. Accompanying disciples who did not recognize him, he who had risen from the dead questioned them and listened at length to their problems before revealing himself. Because, after they said what was on their minds, they were ready to hear what was essential.

What people have to say to us is decisive. But in order for them to dare to tell us something, we must approach them in all simplicity. For them to consider it worthwhile to speak to us, we must rid ourselves of our fine talk and our certitudes. In order to journey with them, we must also sometimes have the courage to say, "I don't know; I don't understand." We will then share their questions, and search for answers together.

Today, in a time of constant change, the church cannot remain above people, or even alongside them; it must be *with* them. Here again Vatican II has shown us the way in its document on *The church in the modern world*: "The joys and hopes, the sorrows and agonies of the men and women of these times are also the joys and hopes, the sorrows and agonies of the church." I can give no better illustration of this vision of the church than these few examples which taught me a great deal:

ANNIE SAW NO WAY OUT of her situation except to have an abortion: Her boyfriend had disappeared, and she had simultaneously lost her job. What kind of a future could she offer her child? Her friends mobilized themselves. They knew how to rally around her, and even succeeded in finding her a job. Because she was no longer all alone, Annie kept her baby.

Others, however, have not found such understanding or practical help within their circle of acquaintances. Should I have condemned them when they came to confide in me? I am no advocate of the abortion pill, despite what has often been written about me, and I believe abortion represents a failure. But should I ignore the agony in which some women find themselves? Should I judge them, blame them, overwhelm them with penances? Or should I try to understand in order to better apprehend the future?

MARC CAME TO TAKE REFUGE in the bishop's residence because he had drunk too much, while his wife and children were expecting him at home. I gave him a cup of coffee and invited him to get warm. Later, he expressed his surprise to members of my ministerial team: "It was funny; the bishop didn't preach at me." Later, on his own, he would talk to me about his family and come to accept his responsibilities.

IT WAS AT THE CHAPLAIN'S OFFICE at the house of detention in Évreux that I met Hervé. He hadn't come to see the bishop. He didn't give a damn about the bishop. The chaplain's office had cake and hot coffee; that's what interested Hervé. We talked. He told me that he lived in two prisons. The one with walls, cells, and bars wasn't the hardest: "If I landed there," Hervé said, "it was because I'd done some stupid things." But there is another prison, "the one we have inside ourselves, that we can never get out of, and which is far more terrible."

We spoke. Often. I did not ask him what he had done or if he was sorry; I didn't give him a missal or a medal of a saint. I don't even know if I mentioned God. Probably I did because, the day after I was dismissed, Hervé who, by strange coincidence, was released the same day, paid me the highest compliment possible during an interview with some journalists: "The Gospel was written for everyone. But when Jacques Gaillot spoke to me about it, I had the impression that it was written just for me, that it pertained to no one but me."

PEOPLE HAVE CRITICIZED ME for not using the word "God" often enough in my speeches. This reached the point that some fanatics even timed me in order to make their case: "You should realize," one of these precise critics told me once, "that in your ten-minute discussion you never once mentioned the name of God!" I told him that one did not bear witness by counting how many times the word "God" is used. The Good News is declared in any genuine human relationship.

Did he understand? Has he really understood that, as the philosopher Simone Weil said, it is not through the way in which someone speaks about God that I can see whether that person has passed through the crucible of divine love, but through the way the person speaks to me about things here on earth?

Face to face with life's victims, I try to focus my attention on their earthly concerns, on their trials and hopes. I dwell on their misfortune, but not on their misconduct. I do not resort to moral preaching. That would be as indecent and as stupid, as are lofty pronouncements on ecology to a starving population that is destroying its environment. Ozone levels, the elimination of forests, and the pollution of the water supply are not urgent concerns for people trying to survive from day to day.

No one can realize to what degree those who are overwhelmed by misfortune suffer from not being heard, from feeling that their complaints or their gestures of revolt disappear into the wind of indifference.

With the prisoner, the very sick, the drug addict, the unemployed, the handicapped person, and at the bedside of all those whom life has excommunicated, there sometimes happens what Francis Thompson wrote about:

> I have searched for my soul, and I have not been able to see it
>
> I have searched for my God, and he has escaped me
>
> I have searched for my brother, and I have found all three.

8

The outcasts first

MY FRIENDS, YOU KNOW my priorities well: Together we are going to fight against destitution, against social and human destitution. Of course, I'm not the only one, praise God! "Many priests put a lot of energy into their work with the outcasts of society," one of my critics said, " but they don't get as much publicity as Jacques Gaillot." True enough. Fortunately for our church, there are numerous priests, as well as men and women religious, who live in constant solidarity with those who are most deprived. They do so with vigor, boldness, and imagination. Then why isn't enough said about them and too much about me? No doubt because I'm a bishop. And apparently I challenge the idea many have of what a bishop is. I'm a surprise, so people talk about me. And of course, I also take a beating.

Abbé Pierre answered the same way when I said to him: "Explain a mystery to me. As soon as I say a word, they pounce on me. You say ten times more, and it gets by quite well."

"First of all," he replied, "it's because I'm not a bishop. In the second place, I believe that the dear Lord has given me an instinct for measured insolence. I have a sense of how loudly I can yell."

From time to time Abbé Pierre has what could be called a healthy rage. He offers an explanation:[8]

> Don't ask me for prudence or careful consideration before taking a decision. And don't ask me to be sensible, either, the way people say to a child, "Be good now; don't move." It's not worth your trouble. I'll never be 'good' in that way. That's the way it is; that's the way I'm built.
>
> Irascibility is one of the human virtues. We generally teach children that anger is a vice, undoubtedly because it makes things simpler. But in that case Jesus was wicked when he overturned the tables of the merchants in the temple. In fact, the capacity for anger is a potentiality, like sympathy or intelligence. What makes it vice or virtue is the object to which it is applied. Notice, for example, how anger can reveal what we love: If I get mad because I have lost a game, it shows that what I love is myself; if I get angry in order

8. *La Testament de l'Abbé Pierre* (Paris: Bayard, 1994).

to protect someone, to rescue someone, such an anger reveals my love for another.

The anger of a bishop, however, has to be more measured. A bishop walks straight; he holds himself erect, in line with the institution.

That became quite evident to me the first time I broke ranks in March 1983: Many people considered that I was not in my place. But I, on the contrary, thought that I ought to be there and not somewhere else. It was at Évreux, during the criminal trial of Michel Fache, a young conscientious objector who was considered a rebel. Once again, I did not choose the occasion, but as I have said, ever since the war in Algeria nonviolence has become one of my principal preoccupations. It seemed to me—and it still seems to me—that it was the role of the bishop to welcome the sensibility that is developing in regard to nonviolence, peace, and disarmament. I attended the trial. Not to make a statement or to protest, but simply to be there, to give silent support to Fache's peaceful struggle.

I was surprised at the reverberations that my presence at this trial produced, and even more so by the controversy that followed. At the same time, however, I quickly realized that part of public opinion had a difficult time accepting the idea that a bishop might find himself on the side of the accused and, by extension, on the side of the down-and-out, the have-nots, and the outcast. Or that he would add his voice to those who cannot be heard or whom others don't wish to hear. As if by acting in this way, I was taking something away from those who have, depriving them of a benefit or a privilege.

I think just the opposite. And the path I have chosen is that of the Gospel: My job is not to convince those who are already convinced, to nurse those who are healthy; I am there to give help to the sick, to extend my hand first to those in despair, to those who are lost, to those who have more need than others of love and comradeship. Whether they are baptized or unbelievers.

In this sense, the Fache trial was a revelation for me. And to some extent it undoubtedly set off everything that followed.

In June 1982 I was welcomed by the Christians of the Diocese of Évreux as "their" bishop. I belonged to them. They deserved me. You haven't had a bishop for twelve hundred years, dear friends of Partenia, and this may be hard for you to grasp, but when those people in the shelter of the cathedral saw me set out to meet the outcasts, the wrecks of society, they didn't understand. What was I doing over there, on the other side, in suspect areas, while they, deserving churchgoers, waited for me?

They complained. I replied that they should address their grievances elsewhere, that I was not the reason for their discontent, and neither was the church. That the person really responsible was someone called Jesus, who had experienced in his flesh the path of abandonment, unjust condemnation, and exclusion.

At the synagogue in Nazareth, taking up the book of the prophet Isaiah, he had proclaimed:

> The spirit of the Lord is upon me;
>   therefore he has anointed me.
> He has sent me to bring glad tidings to the poor,
>   to proclaim liberty to captives,
> Recovery of sight to the blind
>   And release to prisoners.
> To announce a year of favor from the Lord.
>   (Lk 4:18)

Then he added, "Today this Scripture passage is fulfilled in your hearing." All that requires many risks and entails many compromises. We cannot hesitate to get our hands dirty nor want to remain above the battle. I was called, therefore, to bear witness to the Gospel, to everyone and in all places. The lost sheep were my first priority.

After twelve years of life in common with the diocese, I am weak enough to believe that this idea made some progress in the minds of those who were ready to enter into dialogue. In disagreement or not, there is hardly any other way to learn how to become better acquainted or better appreciate each other. Of course, this did not always mean smooth sailing. They were flare-ups, arguments, and misunderstandings. But many understood, and some even followed me.

And then, there was the handful of stubborn people, a hard core, who blocked the Gospel. Those whose letters Cardinal Gantin found on his desk. These people cried scandal and heresy. It seemed inconceivable for them that I should go and concern myself with the damned—the drug addicts, the prisoners, the immigrants, all those fringe people who clutter up the margins of society. That, they were sure, was neither my mission nor my place. They had no problem with an Abbé Pierre, a Guy Gilbert, or many other priests who were "special envoys" concerned with human distress. On the contrary, their commitment, their outcries and protests, were almost unanimously approved among all social classes. That is the privilege—and the weakness—of irregulars, of explorers of the Gospel whose remarkable actions threaten neither the principles nor the functioning of the church. But there always remains the fundamental problem of the outcasts themselves speaking out, and having access to knowledge and responsibility, both in the church and in society. For such justice to be demanded by a bishop—especially by a bishop!—that is what was upsetting.

The responsibility of dragons

HELPING THE DOWNTRODDEN is not enough. Solidarity is not limited to serving soup, handing out shoes, and providing a roof over their heads. Human dignity is nourished by something quite different: for example, by no longer being assisted, by being able to take care of oneself, being responsible for oneself, one's family, one's children. It's there that the task becomes much more complicated, because there are laws—which are frequently tortuous, turned upside down, ridiculed, and buried by insiders. The law on requisition is still in force, isn't it? We have to adapt to it, abide by it. Even if situations have changed. Even in cases of emergency. Even if it means "forgetting" about those who have not been scheduled to be covered by it: Every winter sees the insurrection of the homeless. But which is more illegitimate? To leave thousands of apartments empty of any inhabitants while entire families are on the street, or to put an end to this shameful provocation and requisition the apartments in question, even if the requisition is only an emergency measure while waiting for real arrangements by the government? You know my answer. It is found, with the right to housing, at number seven, rue du Dragon.

But led by the Association Droit and my friends Léon Schwartzenberg, Jacques Higelin, and Albert Jacquard, some people wished to go much further. A living space is not only somewhere where people can eat and sleep. Living space—it seems stupid to have to say it—is a place where one can exist as a human being, with one's responsibilities, duties, distractions, and burdens. To want to create a "people's university," to encourage learning centers, to facilitate fraternal and beneficial contacts between outcasts, artists, and intellectuals, has no other purpose than to permit this awakening, this sense of finally being "someone." But apparently there is something dangerous, subversive, and intolerable in this. "They like us alone, in our corner, hand held out, head bowed, but as soon as we gather together and begin to ask questions, they get frightened," the inhabitants of the rue de Dragon commented with painful irony when they were surrounded by the CRS,[9] who lost a good opportunity to pick up some ideas on a subject that is rarely taught in the barracks.

I didn't have a great deal to add at the time of the trial in the Court of Corrections, which set us against Cogedim, the proprietor of the building on Dragon street. "As long as people simply offer help, there's no problem, but when they see to it that the outcasts raise their head and organize, then it's something else—they're a nuisance."

The church should not lag behind, shouldn't "say things that are so adolescent about the terrible choices that arise in our world" (Gabriel Ringlet). The oppressors, those who snuff out freedom, never wait. They are the first to get involved, the first to take up their position. And if we aren't careful, they occupy the whole area before we can react and push them back.

When I roared out against the new immigration laws in an angry book[10]—which people say (and it's easy for me to believe) played a part in my removal—the Church of France

---

9. The CRS are special police used in disturbances, in especially dangerous situations such as riots or prison revolts. (Trans.)

10. *L'Année de tous les dangers*, in the collection "Coup de Gueule" (Paris: Éditions Ramsay, 1994).

did not appreciate the tone and sense of commitment of my remarks which, it seems, were not those of a bishop. I criticized Charles Pasqua too sharply, and was excessively personal. My criticism seemed to me quite logical, however, since the minister of the interior had become identified for a long time with this policy of closing the borders, and made a major point of it in his election campaign. But I had given offense. The episcopal hierarchy came very close to accusing me of making M. Pasqua unhappy, whereas I naively believed that those who should complain the most were the thousands of men, women, and children who were going to be persecuted by the enforcement of this new law.

It is true that the Catholic Church—less sharply, however, than the Reformed Church—had indicated its disapproval of the law from the beginning, and insisted on proclaiming its solidarity with the immigrants. But wasn't there something better to do than publish a simple text of a few lines? Shouldn't the church have gone further and been stronger? Although the initiative was certainly laudable, there was something improvised and ridiculous about it. In a word, useless. And what is taking place today? One can see the damage that has been done. Every day, we are confronted with heartbreaking cases of couples that have been separated, children snatched from their parents, political refugees returned—in effect, condemned—to their country of origin. Sometimes it is grimly absurd, often it's inhuman, and it's always shameful.

Instead of undergoing such a humiliation in terms of humanity and fraternity, shouldn't the church have fought with greater energy and conviction? Today the cries of alarm raised by the bishops—including Archbishop Duval, president of the assembly of French bishops—about the disastrous consequences of the immigration policy are multiplying. And I tell myself that, apart from questions of form, the official position of the clergy is not very far from my much-publicized howl—whose pages were skimmed with tongs. But the evil was done. The hunt for immigrants is at its height. Too little informed, inadequately motivated, most French people, whether Christians or not, have not sufficiently realized that it is in their country, home of the rights of man, the historical land of asylum, that an ideal of freedom and tolerance is being ignominiously buried. Aren't we, and many others, beginning with politicians, along with many others, in part responsible for such indifference? And for all that, has their own lot—I am speaking of the French— really improved?

DEAR FRIENDS IN PARTENIA, when I say that as an excluded bishop I will be even closer to the excluded, it's not just for the pleasure of a play on words. It is a choice of a man of the church that I made a long time ago. This time, however, they are offering me, if I dare say so, complete freedom.

9 ∼

Powerful images

DEAR FRIENDS IN PARTENIA, I still keep in my heart the most extraordinary collection of powerful images from all those stormy days. But along with that album of unforgettable souvenirs and the breathtaking kaleidoscope of emotions, there appear some more restrained and intimate sketches that are far from being erased from my memory. They are favorite moments which I would like to share with you.

Besides, one asks oneself how it was all possible. I was caught up in a cyclone, tossed about, shaken up, tugged at on all sides, but during the wildest moments, the most frenzied jostling, there was a little digression that held back, for a few precious moments, the crush of events that was trampling everything around.

I see a red rose being held out by an old priest friend. He came from Langres for my farewell mass, and he had just reached the beseiged enclosure of the Jesuit house where, with a few close friends, I had taken refuge before the ceremony. Thirteen years earlier, when I left my diocese in the East, I had performed the same gesture for him—a red rose as a way of saying goodbye.

"Here, I'm giving it back to you," my friend said to me.

I REMEMBER A CUP. It was the one Stephane had received from the minister of youth and sports. On January 22, he presented it to me. Both for him and for me, that cup represented something far different from a trophy.

I had made Stephane's acquaintance in 1992. He was seventeen, and had just lost his brother, who had been killed in his housing project in Sainte-Étienne-du-Rouvray, near Rouen, over a stupid business about a stolen moped. The neighborhood was ready to erupt. Young people were boiling with rage and thought only of vengeance. Stephane wanted to show that other routes were possible. To prove it, he wanted, first, to organize a great festival of hope. He contacted me. I thought it was a fine, comforting idea, remarkable, full of hope. He needed a hall and was running into all kinds of difficulty in obtaining one. I assured him of my support but he wanted more: "I need a written statement. Otherwise, the mayor won't believe me."

I not only filled out the small sheet of paper but promised him that I would come to his festival. It was a huge affair, spreading over several streets around the project. Young people of all origins met and mingled. There was music, dancing, and huge banners; the day was such a success that Stephane was asked to repeat it the following year. And the year after. This time, it was with a gymnasium and a public grant. Meanwhile, deeper contacts were knotted, new projects were launched, and groups were formed.

Stephane was proud of his cup: It represented success and official recognition of his action. Nevertheless, he parted with it. Just to say thank you, to thank an adult who, right from the start, had shown confidence in him. Because Stephane knows that nothing is possible without trust. One day, surely, as precious as that cup is to me, I will in turn offer it to someone else.

ON MY RETURN FROM ROME, prisoners were in the front rank of those who knew how to cheer me up. Their expressions of friendship, their words of hope, and their encouragement took on special value under those difficult circumstances. When one reads the following letter from the inmates of the house of detention in Évreux, things return to their true value. Because they are the ones who suffer— far more than I.

We have at least one point in common. Like us, now you have been excluded. Not for the same reasons, of course. Your crime, if it can be called that, is to have been on the side of the weakest, of the outcast.... You have chosen a different path; you wanted to live Gospel in everyday life.

You have sown panic; you have cracked consciences wide open. It is so difficult to be worthy to serve those who suffer that people have not been able to take it in. You are proud of what you have done and not of what you are. You are not better than others, but what you have done is better than we are. There is neither joy nor peace in a person's conscience if those who suffer the most are not served the first.

There is self-fulfillment only in self-abandonment. The first task of those who wish to act is to lift the veil, to show public opinion what it doesn't want to see. We have saved freedom and justice in law and in theory, but in practice they have the smell of a corpse. We have been taught everything, except the meaning of the human. The destiny of men and women is to be for what is human. Eternal life is not in the future; it is being lived today. In those who suffer there is sanctity.

All this applies to you. Your presence today[11] shows us how humble you are. You honor us; you are our friend, a brother; we will carry your cross with you. The

---

11. I celebrated mass at the prison of Évreux the morning of January 22, a few hours before the rally at the cathedral.

prophet judges the present and sees the future in the light of God. God will recognize his own. . . .

MY LAST DAYS AT ÉVREUX. A priest enters my office with an exultant attitude; he is bringing important news. "At the age of eighty-five, my mother has taken to the streets for the first time in her life. She who had always hidden her rebellion, dared to express herself and protest. She has written a letter to the pope and has joined the demonstration."

Smiling at him, I look over at the cartons that continue to pile up in my office; they are still bursting with letters. The first letters, sent as early as January 13 and 14, were mostly written by young people, expressing their anger with the ardor of twenty-year-olds. Older people confessed that they waited a few days in order to regain a little calm and be able to write with more moderation. All address me as a brother. As if my destitution had brought me closer to them.

Two weeks later, the boxes in the trunk of my car, I set off to see a priest in the Gers area. With a team of volunteers, we set about sorting and classifying this tidal wave of letters. Our purpose was to produce a summary and commentary of all the letters, and send it to each correspondent. As we had done five months earlier, when after Archbishop Duval's warning, thousands of letters of comfort and encouragement had already reached me. Overwhelmed, I asked myself how I was going to respond to all this. Michel

Pinchon, a priest of the diocese, relieved me of the burden, and we sent out a booklet.[12]

That first wave of letters came most often from people who were involved in the church. The reprimand from Archbishop Duval had had a painful impact on them. My personal problem caused them to reflect on their own commitment to the most destitute. This time, the destitute themselves wrote me.

People outside the church and those excluded from society expressed their opinions. Because the sanction I had received was readily understood not just by insiders, but also, crossing the boundaries of the institution, reverberated in every sector of society. "You've been kicked out, just like us," they wrote me.

As for those in the church who are disappointed, they ask themselves, "If they exclude you, who represented the way to our reconciliation with the church, what will become of us?" All those letters were so many SOS appeals sent out to our church and its highest representatives. For this time the questions, criticisms, and complaints were addressed directly to Rome. Directly to the Holy Father.

"I too wanted to write Archbishop Duval," a nun confessed to me last summer, "but I didn't dare address such a

---

12. A special issue of the review *Jésus—les cahiers du Livre Avenir*, edited by "Jonas," an association of priests. It was sent to each correspondent in place of a personal response.

high dignitary. With you, it's not the same." This time they dared to speak, much more loudly. And en masse.

Such boldness clearly indicates the depth of the discontent felt in public opinion. I myself was surprised. When, on January 12, I asked Cardinal Gantin if he had considered the confusion that the proposed sanction would provoke, he answered, "It's not a question of France, but of the church." At that time I had no idea that there would be such a rallying. It's the crowd that made the Vatican budge. It wasn't the ex-bishop of Évreux, or even the emissaries of the episcopal conference who were received at Rome—they were only intermediaries. We are the bearers of a message of pain and revolt from all those who plead for a church more concerned with the human and more anchored in society.

This time, Archbishop Duval was listened to, far more than I had been. In 1989 I had gotten nowhere with my request for an interview with John Paul II. More recently still, when criticized by the episcopal conference, I proposed going to Rome to explain myself, the nuncio had laconically responded, "It's not worth the trouble."

A few weeks later, apparently it was worth it. The special envoys of the Church of France did not come back empty-handed. And I was glad. Just as I was glad at the speed with which echoes of the interview with the pope were made public. It is hardly customary; the religious silence which usually hangs over the debates that go on inside the church not only gives the appearance of artificial unity but is the source of regrettable misunderstandings that make real solutions even more difficult.

This time the mail had not gone by stagecoach. And this quick communication, appropriate for our time, proved that the rumor arrived at the Vatican without losing its force, that those tens of thousands of letters, addressed to bishops, to Rome, and the pope himself, had arrived at their destination. That was good news. The rest followed.

I placed my belongings at 7, rue du Dragon. From Évreux I brought back a television set and a metal file. An icon of the Virgin Mary, a crucifix, a tapestry from Colombia adorn the newly repainted walls. The Emmaüs community lent me a bed and a desk, the desk on which I am writing this letter.

So I became a bishop without permanent residence, a prelate placed on the shelf. Like Paul, "I have learned to be content with the place where I find myself" (Phil 4:11). Friends in Partenia, I know that I can join you no matter when, and that I am also with you among the homeless of the rue du Dragon.

I am waiting. I am in transit. Just like them.

These law-abiding French and foreign families have all benefited from a regular life, with a job and a place to live. And then, one fine day, as a result of some rehabilitation project, they have been thrown out. Naturally, they were on the priority list to return to these handsome new apartments— but for a rent that exceeded their monthly income. And for lack of available apartments within reach, they found themselves back on the street. From an employer's point of view, not having a regular address is a liability, and this is also true for bureaucrats, especially if one is a foreigner—to say nothing of the complications for children in school. All of a sudden, the life of these families was turned upside down. Daily life became an obstacle race. Eviction turned into exclusion. But the DAL transformed their marginalization into a fight for life. A scholar, a professor, a singer, and a bishop served as its spokespersons. What happened to these families could affect anyone. It helped that we were on their side.

To open the door to others is one thing. But it is often a more delicate matter to go to live in someone else's house. The church that preaches welcome ought also to let itself be welcomed. In that way it will change its language, its manner of being, and its liturgy.

THE SUNDAY THAT FOLLOWED my installation at 7 rue du Dragon, I celebrated Mass there. Along with the members of the DAL and neighborhood families, a few friends also slipped in. Some even came from as far away as Belgium. Many didn't know the rituals and prayers, but I could see their emotion. For their benefit, I encouraged everyone present to participate. In particular, each of them spoke up to propose an intention for our common prayer.

It was the second Sunday of Lent, the feast of the Transfiguration. Through Jesus transfigured on the mountain, God shows us humanity as he wants it to be, restored in its eminent dignity. Yes, we are made in his image and like-ness; we are made for Light.

There are moments of perfect happiness, moments when one feels so well, at peace with oneself and with oth-ers. Such moments of fullness exist. They are rare, perhaps, but we have all experienced them. Each of us is capable of living such moments. They continue to send signals to us even when we are in despair. For on the mountain Jesus summons us to the Light.

At the mass I spoke to them also about dignity. It is a good which never disappears, and which each one of us pos-sesses, even if certain people think they have been deprived of it. I told them the story of the man who was selling the paper put out by the unemployed and was interviewed by a TV crew:

"Do you feel that you have regained a certain degree of dignity thanks to this work?" the journalist asked.

"Sir," answered the homeless man, "I have never lost my dignity. It is within me, as it is in you. Let's just say that now people acknowledge it."

No one can take away our dignity. It is part of us.

10 ❧

On the road

DEAR FRIENDS, SHOULD I CONFESS that the joy of meeting you again in Partenia is mixed with a feeling of helplessness? It is almost forty years later, and yet I have the impression that nothing has changed, that evil is constantly present, that goodness has not forced it back one inch. War again bloodies your land and your families. The demon of hatred and intolerance reigns, shattering the hope of a young country that already had so much difficulty getting rid of a regime of oppression and corruption. Yesterday the war was against short-sighted colonialists, overly attached to their privileges. Today it rages in the form of a religious fanaticism with slogans of death and hatred that exploit and distort Islam's true message.

This exploitation of faith has a terrible fascination. Everyone knows that Islamic extremists draw their forces from among the most disadvantaged of the Algerian population. Profiting from the egoism of the well-to-do and the cynicism of the privileged classes, the extremists promise to make up for the deficiencies of the government, as they gather together the abandoned who stagnate in the gutters of society. Especially the young—the most malleable, the most vulnerable, and the angriest.

In an earlier time, religion was nothing less than a comfort against injustice, a remedy to get back on one's feet, a way of affirming one's human dignity and hope for the future. The nurse cares for the wounds of destitution and humiliation. She is available, warm-hearted, and understanding. But as soon as the patient is up again, the nurse gives way to the drill sergeant. That's how Moslem fundamentalism transforms the near-dying of yesterday into the indoctrinated warrior, fanaticized to the point of committing the worst excesses. Even at the cost of life itself.

The damage inflicted by this senseless proselytism is equally visible at the other extreme, where an opposing group of fanatics considers Islam nothing but a religion of cutthroats and the mosque a den of killers. For "true believers" in this deranged jumble of prejudice, everyone who is an Arab hides a razor in his pocket, and everything Moslem is crazy—and anyone who doesn't adopt their radically absurd position is considered suspect.

I myself am suspect. As soon as they see or hear me, those obsessed with the idea of an invasion go back into action, sending me letters that drip with hate and violence. They address me as "Mohammed" Gaillot—as if such a first name was in itself an insult—accuse me of covering up crime, of being a traitor to my country and my religion—in short, as we say during wartime, of having gone over to the enemy.

This is as much as to say that in their eyes the Algerian people as a whole are responsible for the tragedy that bloodies their country, rather than being its victims. This is to forget the calvary of an entire population, taken hostage by the two opposed camps. This is to forget the thousands of innocent people who have been massacred, the blind attempts at assassination and equally blind repression, the tortures and reprisals. This is to forget the amazing struggle by all those who, despite the everyday hell, refuse to submit or to allow themselves to be crushed by the claws of these two opposing forces.

I think especially of those women who demonstrate with their faces uncovered, publicly expressing their choice of a modern and democratic Algeria. Less resigned and fatalistic than the men, they take their position at the outposts, climb the barricades of the opposition, and reject the religious obscurantism of which they are always the privileged victims. Their role is essential in modern Algerian society, and it is undoubtedly for this reason that they are targets of Islamist killers. Kidnapped, raped, and strangled, they still refuse, in spite of the lurking danger, to hide themselves, choosing rather to die or to suffer. They undoubtedly hold the key to the resistance of oppression, and ultimately the key to the future of Algeria.

And we would abandon them in their struggle? Like Pontius Pilate, we would like to wash our hands of the misfortune that threatens a country so dear to us, to which we are attached by so many emotional, historical, and cultural ties. Even worse, we compound the error—refueled by an exaggerated concern for political security—by mixing everything into the the Algerian tragedy. Everything has somehow to be included, everything thrown into the same bag of defiance and hostility. Archbishop Guy Deroubaix,[13] Bishop of Saint-Denis, expressed the same fear:

> It is when we are in trouble that that we know who our real friends are.
>
> It is in the name of this friendship that we are sensitive to what is happening to our brothers: suspicions cast without distinction on an entire people; measures which do not all seem justified; behavior that leads to confusing Islam and terrorism; simplistic judgments which don't take into consideration the political and economic situation linked to today's confrontations between brothers of the same people.

---

13. President of the Bishops' Secretariat for Relations with Islam, Archbishop Deroubaix made this statement August 20, 1994.

In all this, we would like to be attentive to declarations by associations struggling against racism, xenophobia, and exclusivism; to what the Algerian people is saying; to what, in their diversity, believers in Islam are saying; what the Gospel tells us; and to the attitude of our church. We are not free from the confusion between God and the political options that have marked the history of our country.

You know all this, friends in Partenia, as well as I do, if not better. A number of your brothers and sisters who work in France experience it every day, and suffer on the front line from the atmosphere of suspicion that hangs over them without distinction.

One of my friends had a painful experience last summer. Under house arrest at Folembray by order of the minister of the interior, the imam Kechat Larbi was immediately, and without the smallest shred of proof, considered a dangerous individual by part of the French public. I paid him a visit. My detractors again took up their pens: they had seen me shake the imam's hand, a hand stained with the blood of Frenchmen killed in Algeria! Little did it matter to them to know that Kechat Larbi does not support the cause of the Islamic Front, that he is opposed to all violence, that he campaigns for an Islam of peace and tolerance, and that he is among those who see only one way to put an end to the present carnage—negotiation, a rejection of violence, which assumes a return to democracy.

My critics kept up their denunciations: "We didn't see you taking a position when four priests belonging to the White Fathers were killed. "[14]

This was false, of course, but again that didn't seem to matter. I had been interviewed on radio programs and I had protested against that barbarous act. How could it have been otherwise? I am part of the same church in which those four assassinated priests gave witness. But does their murder mean we should kill off interreligious dialogue as well? Are we to submit to the will of criminals, and leave the field open to them? That is exactly what they want . . .

And what the Catholic Church in Algeria rejects. Living twenty-four hours a day in danger of death, and plunged into an atmosphere of extreme nervous tension, priests and men and women members of religious orders there don't allow themselves to be swept away by the tumult. They benefit from double nationality and could return to France without any difficulty. Who would blame them under the present circumstances? But they have chosen to remain and to face the problems. When people are being tested, oppressed, and tortured, that is not the time to abandon them.

---

14. Four White Fathers—three French and one Belgian—were assassinated at Tizi-Ouzou in Kabylia by an Islamic commando group on December 27, 1994.

Addressing the Christians of the country, the Algerian bishops declared: "With you, we wish to pursue the path begun by the Algerian people. It is in this way that we will respond to our vocation."

It is a risky decision, but one adopted with confidence and serenity. The Algerian Church is with its people "in life, and in death." These voices that rise up in this way against violence, that serve both peace and the future, are insufficiently known; it is hard for them to be heard over the cries of hatred.

Their appeals recall another voice. During the 1960s, in the middle of a war that didn't admit its name, the archbishop of Algiers, Léon-Étienne Duval, tried the same approach and showed the same nobility of thought. I was a solider at that time, stationed, as I have said, close to Partenia. And I remember his moving, impressive declarations while, all around him, Algeria was descending into chaos and atrocities.

I think also of another voice from an earlier time, that of Father Charles de Foucauld, whose way of life brought him into such intimate contact with your country. And I ask myself the question: what would he say of today's events, he who had come to love the Maghreb[15] so dearly that he devoted the last part of his life to it?

In his small house made of packed earth in a deserted area of Hoggar, Father de Foucauld put his faith into practice.

---

15. The mountainous coastal region of North Africa composed of Morocco, Algeria, and Tunisia.

He never became comfortable because he remained sensitive to events around him, and allowed them to interrogate him. That is what I have always loved about him. I like the way he had of saying: We are always on the road, we have never completely arrived. This calls for a permanent questioning, which implies that we are envoys, nomads, destined always to go further on.

Father de Foucauld thus became imbued with Moslem culture and mysticism by living like the people of the area and becoming familiar with the habits of their everyday life. He acquired his knowledge of Islam primarily on the human level, and his numerous writings show to what extent this discovery of the Moslem world was able to enrich his faith and spirituality. What would he say, then, he who built a bridge of fraternity between France and the Maghreb, and who, even in his own time, had protested in the strongest terms against the intolerable behavior of certain French servicemen toward the native population? What would he say?

He would undoubtedly be deeply saddened to see his Moslem brothers killing each other. He would suffer and even risk his life for them, whatever group they supported. He would denounce the violence and barbarism on all sides, knowing as we do that they do not lead to any lasting solution. He would condemn terrorism and repression at the same time, struggle against all extreme demands, and campaign fervently for negotiation.

At the same time Father de Foucauld would look further ahead and aim higher. He would try to alert international opinion, and would surely be astonished at the indifference and cowardice of high officials, which is masked by empty statements that carry no real weight. He would wonder about the policy of the French government, which persists in supporting an Algerian government that is riddled with corruption and whose credibility among its own people has been eroded. The voice of the Catholic Church regarding the drama being played out in Algeria would doubtless seem to him too infrequent and too timid.

And surely he would pose this question about a curious fact, a question that others will pose in a few years: How can the institutional church pay such attention to the little incidents of Jacques Gaillot and make a fuss over them, and so discreetly pass over so many tragedies that assault the world?

11 ~

What now?

"HAVE YOU ANY REGRETS?"

The question is clear and direct, yet full of insinuations. The one who asks it—and I was frequently asked, in the aftermath of my transfer—displays, depending on his or her temperament, an appropriate expression. There is in the interviewer's eyes the greedy gleam of someone hunting a scoop, or the melancholy look of a gravedigger who has already measured the coffin.

Do you have regrets? The question could be taken up in a bourgeois perspective: does one miss no longer being snugly surrounded by one's familiar furniture and everyday comfort, in a schedule of customary habits and a framework of security? Partenia, you see, is not and cannot be a life.

The question can also have—and this is more gratify-ing—an intellectual resonance: regret at having gone too far, at having become involved prematurely, at having explored too much of Partenia without being authorized to do so.

Who would not have some regrets? "You must be clever as snakes and innocent as doves" (Mt 10:16). Have I been clever enough? Innocent enough? To maintain an equilibrium on those two fragile ropes is a job for a tight-rope walker, and I suppose that I have not always had the necessary skill. But when a choice becomes necessary, Jesus always prefers gen-uine simplicity to a paralyzing prudence. On my modest level, that was often my situation. And once again, I do not wish to attack the rule that apparently is causing me so much trouble.

Regrets? I have . . . *one*. I regret that I did not commit myself vigorously enough to the causes I was defending. That I did not go further and with less ambiguity on the path that seemed to me both urgent and just. It was a question of temperament, education, and oversight. And equally, of being overburdened. For, in spite of what my detractors pre-tend, my use of my time did not consist in jumping from one airplane into another, in sprinting onto television platforms and signing autographs. The diocese occupied—as is only logical—all my priorities, and the bishop of Évreux did not always have the availability needed for becoming involved in more distant combats.

A bishop who has been "transferred" will not have to present the same excuse. Your mountains of Kabylia, dear friends, dispense me from involvement in local affairs, and Partenia authorizes me to rediscover the path of various actions that I had rather lost sight of, out of obligation.

There is one to which I am especially devoted, and which seems to follow directly as part of the earthly mission of a churchman. It also seems to me that it is an obligation for someone who wishes to believe in a world that would at last be guided by peace and the love of one's neighbor. I refer to nonviolence.

In reviewing all the conflicts that are tearing our planet apart, this is a cause which can easily seem desperate. But is worth the trouble for us to take hold of it without ever getting discouraged. I have already written that the way of hope proceeds by that of nonviolence.[16] This doesn't mean grovelling before power, or giving up the struggle for justice, but instead becoming more bold and courageous. Nonviolence is not nonresistance; being nonviolent does not mean being cowardly or passive, but on the contrary being courageous and active in battle, in order to conquer without being destroyed or destroying others. All this is the complete opposite of the utopian dream mocked by so-called realists who remain undisturbed while the world is transformed into a nightmare.

---

16. *Lettre ouverte à ceux qui prêchent la guerre et la font faire aux autres* (Paris: Éditions Albin Michel, 1992).

The cause of nonviolence against war is that of good against evil. It is a rejection of the charnel houses of Rwanda, the ethnic cleansing in the former Yugoslavia, and the murders in Algeria. It is to make one's own the words of Louis Lecoin:[17]

> If it were proved to me that by making war my ideal would have greater prospects of being realized, I would still say No to war. We cannot build a human society on mounds of cadavers.

NONVIOLENCE DOES NOT MEAN abandoning one's objective and simply becoming resigned. It means fighting, but with the weapons of peace. 1995 is a symbolic date in this struggle: Fifty years ago the cities the Hiroshima and Nagasaki were turned into cemeteries. These two atomic holocausts offered a terrifying idea of the human capacity to produce death. It was such a terrible, enlightening demonstration of this that logically there should not be a sequel. When we're driving and witness an accident, we instinctively become more prudent; our foot presses more lightly on the accelerator. Instead of such a reaction, however, the bomb dropped at Hiroshima has given birth to enough competitors in nuclear armament—sometimes under the pretext of having "a preventive force"—to make

---

17. Louis Lecoin (1888–1971) was a miltant pacifist.

our unhappy planet a dangerous powder-keg. We have brushed against catastrophe on several occasions, while remaining stocked with enough bombs to destroy ourselves many times over; we have left the situation open to the likelihood of even further dangers today as smaller powers hope to imitate the major nuclear powers. In addition, incredible accumulations of money are swallowed up in this race toward suicide, which has until now been avoided. There are even gigantic fairs for scrap iron where missiles and warheads that we no longer know what to do with are left to rust. The result is a traffic in all the components of these engines of death, which are now passed around as post-war surplus. It's a frightful chaos that the sorcerer's apprentice had not foreseen.

Fifty years ago Hiroshima was blown off the map. We are going to see those frightful images again, listen again to unbearable testimonies, and relive the horror of a pulverized city. But Hiroshima—that was nothing, just small-scale work. Since then the forces of destruction have taken giant steps forward, and this terrifying anniversary is the occasion to say with greater force and even greater conviction that nuclear weapons pose a danger to humanity. This Damoclean sword, created by man for the purpose of self-destruction, must be broken and smashed to pieces.

I felt in complete solidarity with Pope John Paul II when he absolutely condemned the conflicts that bloody and dishonor the world today, or when he spoke out sharply against the embargo carried out against a country whose dictator is leading it to ruin.

The embargo concept represents my second regret. I have not made sufficient use of my appearances in the media to explain how much this policy of economic reprisal seems to me both inhuman and cruelly absurd. No one can any longer be unaware of the disastrous consequences it produces on starving populations, on young children who are victims of malnutrition and die by the thousands in hospitals, or of its strategic uselessness. The blockade is nothing more than a taking of hostages, which only penalizes ordinary people. It makes the poor a little poorer, but never affects the elites. The great industrial corporations can take care of themselves; they continue to carry on their affairs, get around the proposed prohibitions, and adapt to the times. Meanwhile the enormous mass of the population bears the yoke of their leaders and the punishment inflicted by the world order. The worst is that we cynically count on a revolt of these beggars—and thousands more deaths—in order to overthrow the existing power, which, well fed and well armed, generally scoffs at all these bold predictions.

Cuba, for example, which since the collapse of the Soviet Union and the end of the cold war can no longer be considered to represent a danger to the United States, has become a vast slum, and Iraq, deprived of its oil trade, has attained a frightening rate of infant mortality. But how are things going for those in power in such countries? Fidel Castro, received at the Élysée with great ceremony, and Saddam Hussein, whose days appeared numbered during the Gulf War but whom no one thinks of overthrowing any longer, have never felt better.

Alas, these are only a few injustices among many. In my room in the rue du Dragon not a day passes without the echo of a painful human drama reaching me, without an appeal for help, without someone writing to me about the wounding of human dignity and the flouting of human rights. I have a lot of time to make up, a great deal of negligence and omission to be pardoned for. I will try from now on to be less often a man who is too busy. I count on you to help me in this.

Dear friends in Partenia, you must realize that I have a strong desire to visit you, to see your faces, to become acquainted with your joys and agonies. Present circumstances prevent me from meeting you. But without waiting, we can begin to work for peace here and now.

༄

TO NOURISH THAT HOPE and that struggle, let the words of Francis of Assisi echo in us:

Lord, make me an instrument of your peace.
Where there is hatred, let me sow love;
where there is injury, pardon;
where there is doubt, faith;
where there is despair, hope;
where there is darkness, light;
and where there is sadness, joy.

Grant that I may not so much seek to be consoled
   as to console;
to be understood as to understand;
to be loved as to love;
for it is in giving that we receive;
it is in pardoning that we are pardoned;
and it is in dying that we are born to eternal life.